Succeeding as a Political Executive:
50 Insights from Experience

Also by Paul R. Lawrence and Mark A. Abramson

What Government Does: How Political Executives Manage

Paths to Making a Difference: Leading in Government

Learning the Ropes: Insights for Political Appointees

Transforming Organizations

Succeeding as a Political Executive:
50 Insights from Experience

Paul R. Lawrence
Ernst & Young LLP

Mark A. Abramson
Leadership Inc.

ROWMAN & LITTLEFIELD PUBLISHERS, INC.
Lanham • Boulder • New York • London

ROWMAN & LITTLEFIELD PUBLISHERS, INC.

Published in the United States of America
by Rowman & Littlefield Publishers, Inc.
A wholly owned subsidiary of The Rowman & Littlefield Publishing Group, Inc.
4501 Forbes Boulevard, Suite 200, Lanham, Maryland 20706
http://www.rowmanlittlefield.com

Unit A, Whitacre Mews, 26-34 Stannary Street, London SE11 4AB

Copyright © 2016 by Ernst & Young LLP

All rights reserved. No part of this book may be reproduced in any form or by any electronic or mechanical means, including information storage and retrieval systems, without written permission from the publisher, except by a reviewer who may quote passages in a review.

British Library Cataloguing in Publication Information Available

Library of Congress Cataloging-in-Publication Data

Lawrence, Paul R., 1956-
Succeeding as a political executive : 50 insights from experience / [by] Paul R. Lawrence and Mark A. Abramson.
    p. cm.
  Includes bibliographical references.
  ISBN 978-1-4422-6929-3 (cloth : alk. paper)—ISBN 978-1-4422-6931-6 (ebook)
  ISBN 978-1-4422-6930-9 (paper : alk. paper): 1. Government executives—United States. 2. Political leadership—United States. : I. Title.
  Library of Congress Control Number: 2016932335

Printed in the United States of America

♾™ The paper used in this publication meets the minimum requirements of American National Standard for Information Sciences—Permanence of Paper for Printed Library Materials, ANSI/NISO Z39.48-1992.

To our wives:

Ellen K. Abramson
Ann P. Lawrence

Contents

Acknowledgments	1
Chapter One: Introduction	3
Who Is the Audience for This Book?	4
What Is the Book Based On?	4
How Is This Book Organized?	6
The EY Initiative in Leadership	7
Part One: The Path to Succeeding	11
Chapter Two: The Right People in the Right Job	13
Insight 1: All Jobs Are Not the Same	14
Insight 2: Match the Right Set of Experiences to Each Position	15
Insight 3: Know That Relevant Experience Really Matters	16
Chapter Three: Getting a Presidential Appointment	19
Insight 4: Understand the Odds of Getting an Appointment	20
Insight 5: There Are Many Reasons to Accept an Appointment	21
Insight 6: There Are Also Many Reasons *Not* to Seek or Accept an Appointment	23
Insight 7: Know What You Are Getting Into	26
Insight 8: Be Prepared to Wait (and Wait)	28
Chapter Four: Between Nomination and Confirmation	31
Insight 9: Be Prepared for Another (Long) Wait	32
Insight 10: Mum Is the Word	33
Insight 11: Spend Time Talking to Your Predecessors	33
Insight 12: Spend Time Seeking Out Information	34
Insight 13: Begin Putting Together Your Team (but Be Patient)	35
Chapter Five: Arriving	37
Insight 14: Have Your Bags Packed, Ready to Go	38
Insight 15: Don't Expect the Red Carpet	39
Insight 16: Beware of (Too Many) Briefings	39
Insight 17: Meet with Career Staff	40
Insight 18: Listen	42
Insight 19: Determine Your Time Frame	43
Chapter Six: Starting	45
Insight 20: Deal with Immediate Problems and Find Out Existing Agency Commitments	46
Insight 21: Assess Your Organization	48

Insight 22: Decide How Many Items on Which to Focus and the Pace of Change — 50

Chapter Seven: Deploying Management Levers — 53
  Insight 23: Reorganize When Needed (But Not as Your First Option) — 54
  Insight 24: Improve Processes and Technology — 56
  Insight 25: Metrics Can Be a Useful Lever — 58

Chapter Eight: Strengthening the Organization — 61
  Insight 26: Enhance Organizational Capabilities — 62
  Insight 27: Strengthen Relationships Inside and Outside of the Organization — 65
  Insight 28: Increase Credibility and Visibility — 68
  Insight 29: Position the Organization for the Future — 71

Chapter Nine: Managing Your Federal Career — 73
  Insight 30: Good Performance Sometimes Gets Rewarded — 74
  Insight 31: Deciding When to Leave Is an Art — 77

Part Two: Succeeding at the Job — 81

Chapter Ten: Succeeding as a Deputy Secretary — 83
  Insight 32: The Job Is Big—Involving Managing Complex Government Organizations — 84
  Insight 33: The Job Contains Ambiguity — 86
  Insight 34: Success Depends on the Relationship with the Secretary — 88
  Profiles-at-a-Glance — 90

Chapter Eleven: Succeeding as a Producer — 97
  Insight 35: Focus on Outputs — 98
  Insight 36: Get the Metrics Right — 99
  Insight 37: Don't Forget the Customer — 99
  Insight 38: Not Everyone Can Be a Producer — 101
  Profiles-at-a-Glance — 103

Chapter Twelve: Succeeding as a Regulator — 109
  Insight 39: Be Prepared for Contention — 110
  Insight 40: Get the Rules Out — 111
  Insight 41: Respond to Unexpected Events — 111
  Insight 42: Don't Forget Your Stakeholders — 112
  Profiles-at-a-Glance — 114

Chapter Thirteen: Succeeding as a Science Executive — 119
  Insight 43: Maintain the Scientific Integrity of the Organization — 120
  Insight 44: Interface with the Political Leadership of the Organization — 121

Contents

Insight 45: Make the Organization Relevant to Government
    Decision-Making ... 121
Insight 46: Reach Out to External Stakeholders ... 122
Profiles-at-a-Glance ... 123

Chapter Fourteen: Succeeding as an Infrastructor ... **127**
    Insight 47: Outreach is Key ... 128
    Insight 48: Get the Money Out ... 129
    Profiles-at-a-Glance ... 130

Chapter Fifteen: Succeeding as a Collaborator ... **133**
    Insight 49: Collaborate with Other Organizations ... 134
    Insight 50: Leverage the Use of Federal Funds ... 136
    Profiles-at-a-Glance ... 137

Part Three: Perspectives from Europe ... **143**

Chapter Sixteen: Insights from European Executives ... **145**
    Succeeding as a Political Executive: Perspectives from Europe ... 146
    Pascal Faure, Chief Executive of the General Directorate for
        Business (French Tax Administration) ... 149
    Jérôme Filippini, General Secretary of the Court of Auditors ... 151
    Dr. Jürgen Gehb, Spokesman of the Board of the German Institute
        for Federal Real Estate ... 153
    Tanja Gönner, Chair of the Management Board of the Deutsche
        Gesellschaft für Internationale Zusammenarbeit GmbH (GIZ) ... 156
    Eric Lucas, General Secretary of the Ministry of Justice ... 159
    Michael Roth, Minister of State for Europe at the German Federal
        Foreign Office ... 161
    Christoph Verenkotte, President of the German Federal Office of
        Administration ... 165
    About the Interviewers ... 170

Index of Interviewers and Interviewees ... **171**

References ... **173**

About the Authors ... **175**

Acknowledgments

In undertaking the fourth volume in our EY Initiative on Leadership book series, there are numerous people to thank for their valuable assistance on this book. We want to first thank the Ernst & Young LLP professionals who participated. We want to thank our European colleagues for their assistance on Part Three of the book: Arnauld Bertrand, Fritjof Börner, Hans-Peter Busson, Birgit Neubert, and Delphine Roy.

We also wish to thank our EY colleagues in the United States who assisted in the project: Allie Cleaver, Katherine Hebert, Kellie Marshall, Meghan Mills, and Sapir Yarden. We want to especially thank the EY government practice leaders who supported this project: George Atalla and Michael Herrinton. Finally, we want to thank the EY support team that assisted us in the review of this volume: Lucia Barzellato, Les Brorsen, Mark Bushell, David Rudd, Jane Spencer, Molly Thompson, and Karon Walker.

Special thanks to former EY colleague Linda Springer for her assistance and support throughout this project. We also benefited from our discussions with Anthony Costa and April Stephenson who shared their insights on government leadership with us.

The book series could not have been completed without our top-notch production team at FIREBRAND. We especially want to thank Sandy Jones for her hard work on the production of all four books. For this book, we were ably assisted by Katie Pyzyk, who edited this volume. We want to thank Jon Sisk and Christopher Utter at Rowman & Littlefield for their valuable assistance. We also want to thank Professor James P. Pfiffner for reviewing sections of this book.

Last, but certainly not least, are the 72 individuals who agreed to be featured in this book and who gave us a substantial amount of their time. It is a true understatement to say there would have been no book series without their participation.

Chapter One

Introduction

Introduction

Who Is the Audience for This Book?

This book is aimed at a very specific audience: new political appointees who will be arriving in Washington throughout 2017 (and beyond) to assume leadership positions in a new administration. Many will come with prior experience in government; others will not have had any public sector experience.

For those with prior federal government experience, they are likely to face a different set of challenges and a different environment than they faced during their previous tenure in government. For those without government experience, they will find government to be dramatically different from their experience in the public, non-profit, or academic sector.

The goal of this book is to speed up the proverbial learning curve of these new political appointees. Only a select number of appointees (mostly cabinet secretaries and a few agency heads) will be fortunate enough to arrive early in a new administration (in January or February 2017). Most other appointees will arrive throughout 2017 (March to December) due to the long and cumbersome confirmation process. They will find themselves playing "catch up" during most of their first year in office. There is thus little time to waste. This book will provide insights from former executives who served during the Obama Administration and a select number of political executives in Europe.

An important, but often unspoken, audience is the many individuals who would like to be considered for a presidential appointment. The book provides management insights as to the reasons why prospective appointees should or should *not* seek or take an appointment.

What Is the Book Based On?

It is based on the real-life experience of 65 high-level executives who served in the Obama Administration, and it is augmented by interviews with seven European political executives. In the United States, most were at the agency head level; from 2009 to 2015, we conducted a series of interviews with these individuals. We interviewed many of them three times during their tenure to better understand their learning curve in real time.

We obtained numerous insights from these political executives during our interviews, based on their real-life experiences in running government organizations. These insights are reflected in the box on the next two pages. The insights presented in this book were tested by political executives who worked hard to be outstanding public servants. We observed first-hand the "life cycle" of political

50 Insights

The Right People in the Right Job
Insight 1: All Jobs Are Not the Same
Insight 2: Match the Right Set of Experiences to Each Position
Insight 3: Know That Relevant Experience Really Matters

Getting a Presidential Appointment
Insight 4: Understand the Odds of Getting an Appointment
Insight 5: There Are Many Reasons to Accept an Appointment
Insight 6: There Are Also Many Reasons *Not* to Seek or Accept an Appointment
Insight 7: Know What You Are Getting Into
Insight 8: Be Prepared to Wait (and Wait)

Between Nomination and Confirmation
Insight 9: Be Prepared for Another (Long) Wait
Insight 10: Mum Is the Word
Insight 11: Spend Time Talking to Your Predecessors
Insight 12: Spend Time Seeking Out Information
Insight 13: Begin Putting Together Your Team (But Be Patient)

Arriving
Insight 14: Have Your Bags Packed, Ready to Go
Insight 15: Don't Expect the Red Carpet
Insight 16: Beware of (Too Many) Briefings
Insight 17: Meet with Career Staff
Insight 18: Listen
Insight 19: Determine Your Time Frame

Starting
Insight 20: Deal with Immediate Problems and Find Out Existing Agency Commitments
Insight 21: Assess Your Organization
Insight 22: Decide How Many Items on Which to Focus and the Pace of Change

Deploying Management Levers
Insight 23: Reorganize When Needed (But Not as Your First Option)
Insight 24: Improve Processes and Technology
Insight 25: Metrics Can Be a Useful Lever

Strengthening the Organization
Insight 26: Enhance Organizational Capabilities
Insight 27: Strengthen Relationships Inside and Outside of the Organization
Insight 28: Increase Credibility and Visibility
Insight 29: Position the Organization for the Future

Managing Your Federal Career
Insight 30: Good Performance Sometimes Gets Rewarded
Insight 31: Deciding When to Leave Is an Art

> **50 Insights** (continued)
>
> **Succeeding as a Deputy Secretary**
> **Insight 32:** The Job Is Big—Involving Managing Complex Government Organizations
> **Insight 33:** The Job Contains Ambiguity
> **Insight 34:** Success Depends on the Relationship with the Secretary
>
> **Succeeding as a Producer**
> **Insight 35:** Focus on Outputs
> **Insight 36:** Get the Metrics Right
> **Insight 37:** Don't Forget the Customer
> **Insight 38:** Not Everyone Can Be a Producer
>
> **Succeeding as a Regulator**
> **Insight 39:** Be Prepared for Contention
> **Insight 40:** Get the Rules Out
> **Insight 41:** Respond to Unexpected Events
> **Insight 42:** Don't Forget Your Stakeholders
>
> **Succeeding as a Science Executive**
> **Insight 43:** Maintain the Scientific Integrity of the Organization
> **Insight 44:** Interface with the Political Leadership of Their Organization
> **Insight 45:** Make Their Organization Relevant to Government Decision-Making
> **Insight 46:** Reach Out to External Stakeholders
>
> **Succeeding as an Infrastructor**
> **Insight 47:** Outreach is Key
> **Insight 48:** Get the Money Out
>
> **Succeeding as a Collaborator**
> **Insight 49:** Collaborate with Other Organizations
> **Insight 50:** Leverage the Use of Federal Funds

executives, from their arrival in government to their departure. We also tracked their tenure in government, as well as their subsequent positions after leaving government service.

How Is This Book Organized?

The book is organized in three parts:
- **The Path to Succeeding** is aimed at all political executives. We believe that the insights in this section can be applied by political executives in all positions throughout government.

- **Succeeding at the Job** recognizes the unique nature of specific types of positions in different types of agencies. All jobs are not the same, as emphasized in Chapter Two. We found that each of the major clusters of agencies provides its leaders with a different set of challenges. We believe the insights in this section will be helpful to political executives in each of the types of agencies we studied during our seven-year project.
- **Perspectives from Europe** presents our interviews with seven political executives in France and Germany. The insights gained from our European interviews are also reflected in Part I.

The EY Initiative in Leadership

This is the fourth book in the EY Initiative in Leadership:
- *Paths to Making a Difference: Leading in Government (First and Revised Edition)* was published in 2011 and 2013. These books were based on our initial interviews with 32 top political executives in the first term of the Obama Administration. The volumes contain profiles of each of the executives interviewed.
- *What Government Does: How Political Executives Manage* was published in 2014. This book was based on interviews with the initial 32 cohorts and 10 additional top political executives not previously interviewed. This volume contains shorter profiles of the each of the executives interviewed, as well as a discussion of the key components of their positions.
- This volume, *Succeeding as a Political Executive: 50 Insights from Experience,* presents the lessons learned from all the political executives we interviewed during the seven years of the EY Initiative in Leadership. Throughout the initiative, we continued to interview more political executives. The final total for the project was 65 political executives who served in the Obama Administration. Several of the executives we interviewed held multiple positions over the course of the Administration. In 2015, EY European colleagues conducted seven interviews with European political executives to test our hypothesis that political executives on both sides of the Atlantic faced similar challenges.

The list of those interviewed for the EY Initiative on Leadership is presented on the following pages.

List of Political Executives Interviewed by Organization*

UNITED STATES

Consumer Product Safety Commission
Inez Moore Tenenbaum, Chairman

Department of Agriculture
Jonathan S. Adelstein, Administrator, Rural Utilities Service
J. Dudley Butler, Administrator, Grain Inspection, Packers and Stockyards Administration
Kathleen A. Merrigan, Deputy Secretary

Department of Commerce
Rebecca M. Blank, Under Secretary for Economic Affairs, Economics and Statistics Administration
Patrick D. Gallagher, Director, National Institute of Standards and Technology, and Under Secretary of Commerce for Standards and Technology
Dennis F. Hightower, Deputy Secretary
David A. Hinson, National Director, Minority Business Development Agency
David J. Kappos, Under Secretary of Commerce for Intellectual Property, and Director, United States Patent and Trademark Office
TJ Kennedy, Acting General Manager, FirstNet
Kathryn D. Sullivan, Assistant Secretary of Commerce for Environmental Observation and Prediction, and Deputy Administrator, National Oceanic and Atmospheric Administration
John H. Thompson, Director, United States Census Bureau

Department of Education
Anthony W. Miller, Deputy Secretary
James W. Runcie, Chief Operating Officer, Office of Federal Student Aid
William J. Taggart, Chief Operating Officer, Office of Federal Student Aid

Department of Energy
Arun Majumdar, Director, Advanced Research Projects Agency-Energy
Richard G. Newell, Administrator, U.S. Energy Information Administration
Daniel B. Poneman, Deputy Secretary

Department of Health and Human Services
William V. Corr, Deputy Secretary
Margaret A. Hamburg, Commissioner, Food and Drug Administration
Pamela S. Hyde, Administrator, Substance Abuse and Mental Health Services Administration
Mary K. Wakefield, Administrator, Health Resources and Services Administration

---

* Titles listed reflect executives' positions at the time of interviews.

Department of Homeland Security
Rafael Borras, Under Secretary for Management
R. Gil Kerlikowske, Commissioner, U.S. Customs and Border Protection
Alejandro N. Mayorkas, Director, U.S. Citizenship and Immigration Services
John T. Morton, Director, U.S. Immigration and Customs Enforcement
John S. Pistole, Administrator, Transportation Security Administration
Leon Rodriguez, Director, U.S. Citizenship and Immigration Services

Department of Housing and Urban Development
Douglas Criscitello, Chief Financial Officer
Brad Huther, Chief Financial Officer
Maurice Jones, Deputy Secretary
David H. Stevens, Assistant Secretary for Housing, and Commissioner, Federal Housing Administration

Department of the Interior
Daniel M. Ashe, Director, U.S. Fish and Wildlife Service
Elizabeth Birnbaum, Director, Minerals Management Service
Michael R. Bromwich, Director, Bureau of Ocean Energy Management, Regulation and Enforcement
David J. Hayes, Deputy Secretary
Abigail Ross Hopper, Director, Bureau of Ocean Energy Management
Marcia K. McNutt, Director, U.S. Geological Survey
Rhea Suh, Assistant Secretary for Policy, Management and Budget

Department of Labor
Erica L. Groshen, Commissioner, Bureau of Labor Statistics
Seth D. Harris, Deputy Secretary
Raymond M. Jefferson, Assistant Secretary of the Veterans' Employment and Training Service
Christopher P. Lu, Deputy Secretary
Joseph A. Main, Assistant Secretary of Labor for Mine Safety and Health

Department of State
Heather Higginbottom, Deputy Secretary for Management and Resources
Thomas R. Nides, Deputy Secretary for Management and Resources

Department of Transportation
Peter H. Appel, Administrator, Research and Innovative Technology Administration
Randy Babbitt, Administrator, Federal Aviation Administration
Michael P. Huerta, Administrator, Federal Aviation Administration
Victor M. Mendez, Deputy Secretary, and Administrator, Federal Highway Administration

Department of Transportation (continued)
John D. Porcari, Deputy Secretary
Peter M. Rogoff, Administrator, Federal Transit Administration
Mark R. Rosekind, Administrator, National Highway Traffic Safety Administration
David L. Strickland, Administrator, National Highway Traffic Safety Administration
Joseph C. Szabo, Administrator, Federal Railroad Administration
Michael Whitaker, Deputy Administrator, Federal Aviation Administration

Department of Veterans Affairs
Sloan D. Gibson, Deputy Secretary
W. Scott Gould, Deputy Secretary
Allison A. Hickey, Under Secretary for Benefits, Veterans Benefits Administration
Robert A. Petzel, Under Secretary for Health, Veterans Health Administration

Executive Office of the President
G. Edward DeSeve, Special Advisor to the President for Recovery Act Implementation
David Mader, Controller, Office of Management and Budget

Federal Energy Regulatory Commission
Jon B. Wellinghoff, Chairman

Office of Personnel Management
John Berry, Director

United States Nuclear Regulatory Commission
Allison M. Macfarlane, Chairman

EUROPE

France
Pascal Faure, Chief Executive of the General Directorate for Business
Jérôme Filippini, General Secretary of the Court of Auditors
Eric Lucas, General Secretary of the Ministry of Justice

Germany
Jürgen Gehb, Spokesman of the Board of the German Institute for Federal Real Estate
Tanja Gönner, Chair of the Management Board of the Deutsche Gesellschaft für Internationale Zusammenarbeit GmbH (GIZ)
Michael Roth, Minister of State for Europe at the German Federal Foreign Office
Christoph Verenkotte, President of the German Federal Office of Administration

Part One

The Path to Succeeding

Chapter Two

The Right People in the Right Job

The Right People in the Right Job

Our key take away from our seven years of research is the importance of getting the right person into the right job. While this may seem obvious, we believe it is the key to success of any administration. There are many components to this simple equation.

The challenge of getting the right people into the right job is the responsibility of the Office of Presidential Personnel (OPP) within the White House. Much work on potential appointees, however, will take place prior to the formal establishment on a new OPP on January 20, 2017. The identification of potential appointees is likely to occur throughout the presidential campaign. The hard work of vetting, selecting, and nominating the first wave of presidential appointees will take place during the president transition from November 9, 2016, to January 20, 2017.

Based on our research and interviews, we believe understanding the following insights is crucial to the success of the president's personnel operation:
- **Insight 1:** All jobs are not the same
- **Insight 2:** Match the right set of experiences to each position
- **Insight 3:** Know that relevant experience really matters

Insight 1: All Jobs Are Not the Same

In order to succeed in getting the right person into the right job, the Office of Presidential Personnel must fully understand that all jobs are not the same. Each position has different experience requirements.

There are indeed several different ways to distinguish jobs that can assist OPP in making selections:
- **Is it a policy or management position?** A key first step is determining whether the predominant activity of the position is "making policy" or "managing an organization." While those running organizations are frequently involved in policy-making, the skills and background needed for managerial positions are significantly different than those in policy positions.

  Our research makes an important distinction between "policy" jobs and "management" jobs. Our research focused on management positions. While many come to Washington to "do policy," much of agencies' work is about executing—not making—policy.

  The concepts of a "policy person" and a "managerial person" are archetypes that can be used in sorting candidates for the right job. A policy person is clearly appropriate for the position of Assistant Secretary for Planning and Evaluation (ASPE) in the Department of Health and Human Services. Based on our observations over the years and research conducted for this book, a managerial person faces a high probability of being frustrated by "all the talking and debating" in a policy job.

Conversely, a policy person may find a managerial position frustrating. Managers, in contrast, find great satisfaction in serving in agencies where there are clear objectives and performance data. As William Taggart, former Chief Operating Officer, Office of Federal Student Aid, Department of Education, put it, "There are two separate sets of skills—the implementers are not the policy folks, and the policy makers are not implementers."

Maurice Jones, former Deputy Secretary, Department of Housing and Urban Development, came to a similar conclusion to Taggart. Jones says, "The problem is that people don't come to the federal government to do execution…You can have the greatest, most innovative policies ever, but without execution, these policies can't succeed."

- **If it is a management position, what type of organization is it?** Based on our research, we found it helpful to distinguish among the following types of agencies:
  — **Production agencies:** These agencies have clear deliverables to the public, such as providing student loans, veterans' benefits, and transportation security.
  — **Regulatory agencies:** These agencies regulate the nation's safety and health and include agencies such as the Food and Drug Administration and the Consumer Product Safety Commission.
  — **Scientific agencies:** These agencies conduct the nation's research and development and include agencies such as the National Institutes of Health, the U.S. Geological Survey, and the National Institute of Standards and Technology.

Insight 2: Match the Right Set of Experiences to Each Position

One of the crucial roles of OPP is determining the set of experiences most needed in a specific position at a specific point in time. There is no doubt that nearly everyone on the long list for a presidential appointment is clearly qualified, in the sense of having a distinguished professional career and impressive educational credentials. But the key question is whether the person has the right set of experiences for a specific job at the point in time when she or he is selected.

An example of changing the desired set of experiences for a job is the White House decision in 1998 to seek a "manager" as the head of the Internal Revenue Service (IRS). Throughout its previous history, the IRS had always had a distinguished tax lawyer as its head. In 1998, a decision was made to look for a business executive who would be able to manage the information technology challenges then facing the IRS; Charles Rossotti was selected. The right set of experiences had changed for the IRS. In 2013, President Obama nominated another individual with extensive business experience, John Koskinen, to serve as IRS commissioner.

Another example of the White House deciding on a new set of desired experiences for a position was the selection of Michael Bromwich to take over the Department of the Interior's Minerals Management Service (MMS) in the aftermath of the 2010 Deep Horizon crisis in the Gulf of Mexico. Instead of seeking an individual with the traditional set of energy and natural resources experience for MMS, a decision was made to recruit an executive with crisis management and turnaround skills. In addition, at that point in the history of MMS, it was appropriate (and perhaps necessary) to select an individual who had *not* had previous experience with the energy industry.

Insight 3: Know That Relevant Experience Really Matters

After coming to agreement on the right set of experiences, the next challenge facing OPP is finding individuals with "deep" experience. While individuals can "learn on the job," it is essential to find individuals with relevant experience to the job being filled.

An additional challenge for the OPP is anticipating problems ahead of time and making selections partly based on the question, "What type of individual and what type of experience would be necessary if the agency faced a major crisis?" In the case of the Department of Labor's Mine Safety and Health Administration, Administrator Joseph Main had the prior experience to deal with the Upper Big Branch mine explosion that occurred in 2010. Main recalls, "I've lived through these experiences before, so I knew what to expect ... My experiences earlier in my career were crucial." Main began working in coal mines in 1967. In 1974, he joined the staff of the United Mine Workers of America, where he spent his career on safety-related issues. He had been involved in responding to the 2001 Jim Walter mine explosion and the 1984 Wilberg Mine explosion. So when the Upper Big Branch explosion occurred, Main knew what needed to be done because of his participation in previous mine explosions.

The need for relevant experience was emphasized by Michael Whitaker, Deputy Administrator, Federal Aviation Administration, Department of Transportation. He cautioned that individuals accepting positions (or offered a position) must have the right experience for jobs in government. "These are really big organizations to run," comments Whitaker.

Another good example of experience making a difference is Edward DeSeve, former Special Advisor to the President for Recovery Act Implementation. In describing starting his new position overseeing the implementation of the American Recovery and Reinvestment Act (Recovery Act), he recalls, "I just dug in and got started. I had my experience as the Deputy Director for Management in the Office of Management and Budget, so I knew what to do."

There are many other examples indicating relevant experience really matters. David Stevens, former Assistant Secretary for Housing, and Commissioner,

> **Not a Good Fit: The Case of Michael Brown**
>
> While there are probably numerous cases of "bad fits" for key managerial positions, they seldom become publicly acknowledged and receive national publicity. When a "bad fit" does receive national attention, it does not reflect well on the administration that appointed the individual. This was certainly the case with Michael Brown, former Administrator, Federal Emergency Management Administration (FEMA).
>
> Brown's performance during Hurricane Katrina received much attention during the immediate aftermath of the hurricane, and he resigned shortly after the crisis. In his book, *The Great Deluge: Hurricane Katrina, New Orleans, and the Mississippi Gulf Coast,* Douglas Brinkley comments on Brown's experience for the position of FEMA Administrator:
>
>> By all accounts, Michael Brown was an unlikely head of an emergency organization like FEMA…Nothing in Brown's resume…recommended him to lead America's disaster relief efforts. (pages 245–246)
>
> Unlike Brown, the FEMA administrators who followed him all had extensive experience in emergency management. President George W. Bush appointed Robert D. Paulison as FEMA administrator in September 2005, replacing Brown. Paulison had previously served as head of the United States Fire Administration and the Directorate of Preparedness. Prior to his federal experience, Paulison served as fire chief of Miami-Dade Fire Rescue. He was responsible for the cleanup after Hurricane Andrew in 1992.
>
> President Barack Obama appointed W. Craig Fugate as FEMA administrator in May 2009. He now has the second longest tenure of any FEMA administrator. Prior to his appointment, Fugate was director of the Florida Emergency Management Division, where he coordinated the state's response to seven major hurricanes, including Hurricane Katrina.
>
> There is wide agreement that one of the lessons learned from the federal government's response to Hurricane Katrina is that experience matters.

Federal Housing Administration, Department of Housing and Urban Development, spent the early part of his career as a loan officer and had extensive experience in the banking industry. David Kappos, former Under Secretary of Commerce for Intellectual Property, and Director, United States Patent and Trademark Office (USPTO), Department of Commerce, spent his career working closely with USPTO and the intellectual property community to improve the patent application process. Both William Taggart, former Chief Operating Officer (COO), Office of Federal Student Aid (FSA), Department of Education, and current FSA COO James Runcie's careers in the banking industry served them well in working with the student loan "ecosystem," which includes the lending industry in a key role. Allison Hickey, former Under Secretary for Benefits, Veterans Benefits Administration (VBA), Department of Veteran Affairs, had spent 27 years in the military and had firsthand experience with the Department of Veteran Affairs as a retired military officer. John Pistole, former Administrator, Transportation Security Administration, Department of Homeland Security, had firsthand experience in airline safety as Assistant Special Agent in Charge, Boston. While in that position, he helped lead the investigation and recovery efforts for the Egypt Air Flight 990 crash off the coast of Rhode Island. So when it came to understanding the activities of their organizations, all had firsthand experience on the front line and understood the management challenges facing them.

Chapter Three

Getting a Presidential Appointment

Getting a Presidential Appointment

Throughout 2016 (as well as 2017, and beyond), many previous appointees and prospective appointees will begin thinking about whether they might get a phone call from the transition team or the Office of Presidential Personnel asking about their interest in serving in the new administration. Regarding the "phone call," we gained five key insights for prospective appointees from our research and interviews:
- **Insight 4:** Understand the odds of getting an appointment
- **Insight 5:** There are many reasons to accept an appointment
- **Insight 6:** There are also many reason *not* to seek or accept an appointment
- **Insight 7:** Know what you are getting into
- **Insight 8:** Be prepared to wait (and wait)

Insight 4: Understand the Odds of Getting an Appointment

Getting a presidential appointment is hard. The odds are against you. From the start, it is important for prospective appointees to keep their expectations realistic. There are many highly qualified individuals all eager to come to Washington and getting a presidential position is a long shot. Working for the winning presidential candidate during the campaign or having outstanding credentials is no guarantee for getting a position (though both might help).

The reality is that there are not that many political positions available to a new administration. Washington is really a career town; the number of career civil servants is far larger than the number of political appointees. In some agencies, the numbers are dramatic. As a rule, the more technical the agency, the fewer the number of political appointees. One agency head tells us, "I'm the only political appointee. This largely is a career agency."

We were told numerous times that the number of political appointees in many agencies is very small:
- Michael Huerta, Administrator, Federal Aviation Administration (FAA), Department of Transportation (DOT), says, "There are only six appointees in the agency. We need career leadership to run the agency. There is not a bright line between our political folks and our career folks." There are currently over 47,000 employees in the FAA.
- Peter Appel, former Administrator, Research and Innovation Technology Administration (RITA), DOT comments, "We don't have many political appointees—just the deputy administrator and general counsel." RITA has over 4,000 employees.
- Abigail Ross Hopper, Director, Bureau of Ocean Energy Management (BOEM), Department of the Interior, had a similar observation. In describing her arrival at the agency, she recalls, "I was impressed with the professionalism

> ### Types of Presidential Appointments
>
> Washington is famous for acronyms and the first set of acronyms that prospective appointees must know and understand is the types of political appointments available. There are four basic types of appointments that a political appointee can receive:
> - **PAS: Presidential Appointment with Senate Confirmation.** According to the 2012 edition of *The United States Government Policy and Supporting Positions* (more commonly known as the *Plum Book*), there are 1,141 PAS positions. This number is misleading, however, because it includes part-time positions to presidentially appointed boards and commissions. A more commonly accepted figure is that there are between 700 and 800 executive-level positions to be filled.
> - **PA: Presidential Appointment without Senate Confirmation.** The 2012 *Plum Book* lists 314 PA positions.
> - **SES: Non-career Positions in the Senior Executive Service.** The federal Senior Executive Service consists of roughly 7,000 career and political executives. The legislation establishing the SES mandated that no more than 10 percent of those positions could be political appointments, so about 600 to 700 non-career SES members are available to a new administration.
> - **SC: Schedule C Excepted Appointment.** These are lower-ranking positions in the General Schedule (GS 6-15) that can be political appointments. The 2012 *Plum Book* lists 1,559 Schedule C positions. They are usually reserved for special assistant-type appointments.
>
> Thus if you aspire to an agency head position or an assistant secretary level position, you must realize that there are only 700 to 800 of these top level positions. As discussed in Insight 4, the odds are against you in getting one of these "plum" positions due to the very large number of highly qualified candidates and the relatively small number of positions.

of the BOEM staff. This is largely a career agency. There are only two political appointees in the agency. The career staff explain how the Bureau works."

As seen in the *Types of Presidential Appointments* box above, the numbers are not encouraging and should give prospective appointees pause before assuming their credentials will easily land them a "plum" position in Washington.

It should be acknowledged that there is an important exception to the "long shot" nature of getting a president appointment. Arne Duncan, former Secretary of the Department of Education, recalls, "I definitely didn't want to come to Washington. I came here because my friend became the president...And it was just a crazy chance of a lifetime to try and have an impact" (Layton 2015).

Insight 5: There Are Many Reasons to Accept an Appointment

We were impressed with the reasons that the individuals we interviewed gave us in describing why they decided to come (or come back) to Washington. The reason most cited was that the job offered an opportunity to make a difference and they felt they had a unique opportunity to contribute to the organization they were asked to lead.

In many cases, these individuals had previously served in government and were part of the professional community surrounding the agency they were being asked to lead. In the case of John Thompson, Director, U.S. Census Bureau, Department of Commerce, he had previously served at the Census from 1975 to 2002 in senior positions, including leading the 2000 Census. After leaving the Census in 2002 to join the National Opinion Research Center, he served as a member of the Committee on National Statistics at the National Academy of Sciences, and as a member on the panel to review the 2010 Census. When offered the position of director in 2013, Thompson recalls, "I wanted to see what changes I could bring to the Census. I believed we could save money on the 2020 Census. I felt that the 2020 Census clearly needed a conceptual vision."

Huerta had a similar experience at the FAA. After having served as deputy administrator from June 2010 to December 2011, and acting administrator starting in December 2011, Huerta recalls, "In the spring of 2012, former Secretary Ray LaHood asked me to consider being nominated as administrator. We had a good conversation. I had to talk to my wife about accepting the nomination. I knew that this was an important time for the agency. I viewed it as a 'call to serve.'"

Mark Rosekind, Administrator, National Highway Traffic Safety Administration (NHTSA), Department of Transportation, also concluded that it was a critical time period in which to lead. He recalls, "I had just finished five years at the National Transportation Safety Board. My background is in safety, so I understood the issues facing NHTSA. It was a crucial time for the Agency. The Agency was in the middle of the Takata airbag problems and the General Motors situation. I came to NHTSA with a two-year expiration date (the end of the Obama Administration), so everybody knew we had to move quickly. Time was of the essence and we needed to get things done."

In addition to meeting the challenges of a specific agency during a specific period of time, there is also the call to public service. Nearly all of the political executives we interviewed strongly endorsed answering the call to service. Margaret Hamburg, former Commissioner, Food and Drug Administration, Department of Health and Human Services, says, "I would encourage people to come into public service. You cannot always accomplish everything you want, but you can have an impact. You can gain different perspectives and have an extraordinary experience. You need commitment and a passion for the work."

John Morton, former Director, United States Immigration and Customs Enforcement, Department of Homeland Security, echoed Hamburg. He says, "Public service is very rewarding. You are motivated every day. You are doing right and serving people. I would recommend public service without reservation. Individuals should do public service for the right reasons. They have to be motivated to take on an organization and believe in its mission. You have to get it right and come for the right personal reason. You are asking people in the agency to follow you into the trenches."

Insight 6: There Are Also Many Reasons *Not* to Seek or Accept an Appointment

Thompson, Huerta, and Rosekind all believed they were the right person at the right time, and they could each make a contribution to their organization. But it does not always work out that way. Some individuals end up accepting appointments for which they may not be the best fit. Individuals may not be offered their first choice (or even their second or third) and thus face the dilemma of taking a job that might not be a good fit.

While much of the focus is on accepting a position, not enough attention is given to a discussion of why *not* to seek or accept a position. There are a variety of reasons for *not* accepting a specific position. In deciding whether to pursue (and ultimately accept) a presidential appointment, an individual must answer the following questions:

- Does my experience prepare me for the job? (The experience fit)
- Is this the "right" job for me? (The job fit)
- Does the job fit my personality and work style? (The personality fit)
- Am I willing to subject myself (and my family) to the scrutiny of the nomination process? (The scrutiny fit)

The experience fit. While people might be unwilling to admit (either prospectively or in hindsight) that their experience does not prepare them for the job they are seeking or have taken, we believe that individuals considering an appointment should ask themselves the following questions:

- What is your experience dealing with the mission of the organization to which you are seeking an appointment?
- What is your relevant management experience?
- Do you have honed and tested management and leadership experiences that will instill confidence in your agency?
- Do you have a plan to be successful in the job?
- Are you prepared if something goes horribly wrong?
- Do you have experience dealing with a crisis that could happen during your tenure?

The decision to accept (or even seek) a presidential appointment is clearly a difficult one involving many professional and personal considerations. In making the decision to seek or accept an appointment, there is one overarching question that each prospective appointee must ask: Is this the right position for me? Determining whether the position is the right fit for oneself is crucial to ultimate success in office. During this project, we interviewed political executives who regularly drew on prior experiences to help them do their jobs. Their prior experience put them much further ahead than those who lacked experience. If you are considering a position for which your answers to the previous questions are "no" and you believe you will be able learn it all on the job, be advised that this is a high-risk path.

The job fit. If you do decide that your experience fits the job, the next key question is whether the specific position offered is the "right" job for you. While past and present position appointees often are reluctant to admit that they were appointed to the "wrong" position, there is much anecdotal evidence of people changing jobs to find the right fit. As discussed earlier, this is especially true of "management" people who are in placed in "policy" positions (or vice versa). There are two interesting examples of this phenomenon. After serving for four years as director of the Office of National Drug Control Policy (ONDCP), R. Gil Kerlikowske was asked for recommendations to head the Department of Homeland Security's U.S. Customs and Border Protection (CBP). Kerlikowske recalls, "After being asked for recommendations, I volunteered myself to head CBP. I was eager to get back into operations and get away from policy. I was familiar with Southwest border issues." Kerlikowske had spent his career in law enforcement, including serving as chief of police in Seattle, Washington, prior to accepting the position at ONDCP.

Ray Kelly, former police commissioner of New York City, had a similar experience during his tenure in the federal government. During the Clinton Administration, Kelly was selected in 1996 to serve as under secretary for enforcement in the Department of the Treasury. In that job (prior to the creation of the Department of Homeland Security), Kelly was responsible for overseeing the Secret Service; the Bureau of Alcohol, Tobacco, and Firearms; the Customs Service; the Office of Foreign Assets Control; the Financial Crimes Enforcement Network; and the Federal Law Enforcement Training Center. In 1998, the position of commissioner of the customs service became vacant. Under Secretary Kelly had set up a committee of three assistant Treasury secretaries to collect resumes, interview candidates, and settle on three finalists for the customs position. Kelly then passed on the three names to Secretary of the Treasury Robert Rubin who didn't like any of them. In his memoir, *Vigilance: My Life Serving America and Protecting Its Empire City,* Kelly recalls,

> I thought about what to do next. Should we start the process over again? Should we round up more candidates? Should we take a second look at some of those who didn't make the round of the finalists?
>
> It seemed like an interesting job. The Customs commissioner was responsible for twenty thousand employees, 328 ports of entry, and an agenda of challenging issues such as personnel search.
>
> "What about me?" I asked Rubin when I went to his office to discuss the matter.

"Let me think about that," he said.

As he reflected, I proposed this scenario: promote James Johnson from assistant secretary to undersecretary...He and I would swap levels. Instead of him reporting to me, I'd report to him.

Rubin went for the idea, and it worked for me. I had learned that I was much better suited for running an operational agency like Customs than being inside a sprawling, multilevel oversight bureaucracy. What I enjoyed most – and what I was best at, I thought—was rolling up my sleeves and running things, not being three or four levels removed... (pages 124-125)

The Ray Kelly case does raise the interesting question of how "high" a position an individual should seek. Several of the executives we interviewed mentioned that one of their criteria in accepting a position was whether it was "big" enough to make a difference. Some individuals concluded that a position might be "too low" in the hierarchy to make the impact they sought. Thus, the "job fit" question has several interesting components to it.

In addition to their desire to return to operations, it is also worth emphasizing that both Kelly and Kerlikowske had extensive operational experience. A related observation is that individuals without operational experience frequently have difficulty in these type positions. Those with experience doing policy work often underestimate the different skills needed to perform operational positions. Successful "operations" political executives frequently have deep experience in running organizations that is quickly transferable to managing in the federal government.

The personality fit. Some people are not well-suited for bureaucracy (in either the public or private sectors). Bureaucracies move slowly, with many obstacles standing in the way of a specific goal. In reflecting on his government service, Michael Whitaker, Deputy Administrator, FAA, DOT, advises, "For some people, they will find that government does not move fast enough for them. Some people should not come to government if they are not going to like the speed of it."

Nearly all those interviewed commented on the speed (or more accurately, the lack of speed) in government. While she is very much enjoying her current position, Heather Higginbottom, Deputy Secretary of State for Management and Resources, Department of State, notes, "I have found that everything takes more time than I had anticipated. Many different entities need to be involved so that we are addressing all aspects of an issue, and that requires lots of sign-offs. It takes a lot of time, but it also ensures coordination and diversity of perspectives."

Erica Groshen, Commissioner, Bureau of Labor Statistics, Department of Labor, commented on the speed of change, "I do get frustrated with the pace of change. But I know that changes take time to make. For example, if we wanted to make a change in the Consumer Price Index, we have to make sure we get it right. Too much depends on getting the number right, since a 0.1% mistake would cause a $1 billion over or underpayment of Social Security benefits. We want to be innovative and flexible, but we cannot be cavalier. We must do things in the proper way, and that often slows things down."

You get the idea. While a crisis might speed up the bureaucracy, government requires patience and a long time frame. Quick hits are possible, but they are the exception rather than the rule. Prospective appointees need to understand their temperament and style. There is room for some entrepreneurship in government, but again it is the exception rather than the norm.

The scrutiny fit. Finally, prospective appointees have to decide whether they wish to make their lives an "open book"—both literally and figuratively. An FBI investigation is required for all appointees, as well as intense scrutiny of an individual's financial situation. All financial forms required by the Office of Government Ethics and congressional committees are made public. Some of the individuals we interviewed recalled the costly process of having accountants assist them in the preparation of their disclosure forms.

In addition to the individual under consideration, that individual's family might also come under public scrutiny. In some instances, the press might report on a family member that has come to its attention.

The entire career of an individual being nominated for a position also comes under the microscope. It is now common for controversial incidents from the past to receive renewed attention. In the age of the Internet, it is not very difficult to find past speeches and comments to the press that can be raised in a congressional hearing. During the confirmation hearings of former Secretary of Defense Chuck Hagel, his previous comments on a range of issues were raised and had the potential to jeopardize his confirmation. When asked to comment on the confirmation process, one of our interviewees said, "I certainly wish I had written fewer articles over my career."

Insight 7: Know What You Are Getting Into

The stakes are high in accepting a presidential appointment. While many appointees leave Washington with their reputations enhanced, there is also the risk of leaving Washington with a damaged reputation. This (usually) occurs not based on personal misbehavior but instead on poor agency performance or a major crisis happening on one's watch.

While a crisis cannot always be predicted, you can do the following:
- Assess the "state" of the organization
- Assess your comfort level with your future colleagues

The state of the organization. Before accepting the position, you must understand the "state" of your organization and the challenges you will be confronting. As part of your initial research on your prospective organization, you should find out whether the organization is on the Government Accountability Office

> ## The Nomination Process
>
> - **"Early" conversations.** Many individuals will have conversations with key officials about potential appointments. These conversations might occur with the Office of Presidential Personnel or a new cabinet secretary's key staff. The amount of hiring discretion given to a cabinet secretary will vary greatly from administration to administration, and even within an administration (some cabinet secretaries may get hiring authority during their own conversations with the president and his staff, while other cabinet secretaries will not). These early conversations often turn out to be just a conversation and there is no follow-up. If the conversation does indeed go well, there is often a substantial wait to hear back on next steps for a potential appointment.
> - **Internal White House vetting.** This is often described as a "black box." We know that FBI clearance is required, as well as the review of financial forms. In recent years, this process has increased in length of time due to both the backlog in the number of individuals to be reviewed, as well as concern not to make a mistake. There will also be extensive conversations during this time period, including interviews with key departmental officials as well as White House staff.
> - **Intent to nominate.** After internal White House vetting and approving the nomination to go forward, the White House will announce an "intent to nominate" a specific individual. This, however, is prior to the White House sending the official nomination papers to the Senate for its review. This is often a time-consuming task.
> - **Nomination sent to the U.S. Senate.** After it reaches the U.S. Senate, the appropriate Senate committee (or subcommittee) will undertake its own review of the nominee's background and financial forms. Hearings will be held. After the hearing, the nomination will go to the appropriate subcommittee and then to full committee for a vote. After the committee vote, the nomination (provided that a "hold" is not placed on the nomination) goes to the Senate floor for final approval. In recent years, the nomination process has become highly charged and highly contentious. It is unclear what degree of partisanship will face the next administration and whether the confirmation process will proceed at a faster pace than in recent years.

(GAO) High Risk List. If the agency is on the high risk list, that will tell you much about the challenges you will be facing. Also, find out whether you will be administering a new piece of legislation, a new set of regulations, or both.

In many ways, you need to undertake your own informal risk assessment of the position. While we are not recommending that you automatically turn down a position in an agency with performance problems, we are recommending that you be fully aware of the challenges facing your prospective organization. While your "deep dive" into the agency will occur after you arrive at the agency, you do want to find out if there any obvious, well-known problems you will be facing if you accept the position.

William Taggart, former COO, Office of Federal Student Aid (FSA), Department of Education, describes the process he undertook to assess FSA: "As a former management consultant, I knew how to assess organizations. Therefore, I had a good idea of the situation I was walking into. I began discussions with the department in February 2009. By late February, I had a meeting with Tony Miller, who was then a special assistant to Secretary Arne Duncan. We reviewed the challenges and expectations of FSA and the COO role. Secondly, all the previous FSA annual reports and strategic plans were available on the Internet. Those documents gave me a lot of insight about the organization. Lastly, I read about the pending legislation that would substantially change the way FSA operated. All of these sources of information helped me to obtain a clear view on the current state of affairs at FSA. After careful consideration, I determined that I was well suited for this type of leadership challenge."

Comfort level with future colleagues. During your initial conversations about potentially accepting a position in a new administration, it is important to assess your comfort level with your future colleagues. In those instances where you have worked with prospective colleagues in the past, during the presidential campaign, or the transition, you will already have a good sense of your comfort level with future colleagues.

In some instances, you will be working with colleagues whom you do not know. Rebecca Blank, former Under Secretary for Economic Affairs, Department of Commerce, had a series of conversations with her future colleagues. "I was impressed by the people on the fifth floor, the Secretary's office," recalls Blank. "I was impressed with them when I interviewed for the job. And I continued to be impressed with them when I got here. It's a superior group of people. The quality of these folks is one of the reasons I took the job."

Your success will depend, in part, on your ability to work effectively with colleagues. A good chemistry between you and your boss is crucial, as are good working relationships with your fellow political executives. If red flags appear during your interview process, you should take heed and make it part of your internal risk assessment to determine whether this position or agency is the place for you. Good chemistry is especially critical in the relationship between the secretary and deputy secretary as described in Insight 34 on page 88.

Insight 8: Be Prepared to Wait (and Wait)

If you decide you are interested in an appointment and you have answered affirmatively the questions posed on the previous pages, the next stage is to begin the waiting game. For every political appointee, there is a different, unique story as to how she or he landed his or her Washington position. Each new administration designs its own presidential appointment process. In recent years, the two candidates for President have established early transition offices during the spring, summer, and fall of the presidential campaign that allow them to undertake some preparation for assuming office. During this period, lists of potential candidates for appointments begin to be developed. The lists grow exponentially after the election during the official transition period between Election Day and January 20.

There is a clear hierarchy in which appointments get filled first and sent to the United States Senate for confirmation (after extensive internal vetting by the transition office). White House staff and cabinet secretaries usually have been named during the November to January transition. Confirmation hearings on cabinet secretaries are often held in January and February. After confirmation, cabinet secretaries arrive at their departments with skeletal political staffs, usually consisting of Schedule C special assistants.

David Stevens, former Assistant Secretary for Housing, and Commissioner, Federal Housing Administration, Department of Housing and Urban Development (HUD), describes his experience waiting for confirmation, "I arrived at HUD in July 2009 after being nominated in April 2009. I started talking to Secretary Shaun Donovan about this position in February (2009). The appointments process was slow. It's never quick. You have the White House review, the FBI review, and the financial review. It's a long process."

This experience is somewhat typical for an administration's first year. The spring and summer of 2009 were a busy time for new arrivals to the Obama Administration. About one-third of our interviewees arrived in May 2009, after the Senate undertook a flurry of confirmation activity to complete action on a large number of nominees prior to its June recess. In July and August 2009, another one-third of our first round of interviewees were confirmed and began their new duties.

During a president's second term, appointee selection, nomination, and confirmation can take much longer. One of the political executives we interviewed in 2014 described his experience to us: "While I was in my previous [private sector] position, I had begun talking to the Administration about a position. I told them I would be interested in a job if I was convinced that I could make a difference… In May 2013, I was approached for my present position and I took the job. I thought it was a daunting challenge. But I felt I could make a difference in this job. I then met with the secretary and he told me that I was the guy he wanted. My nomination was announced in early November 2013. I was then confirmed in February 2014."

Chapter Four

Between Nomination and Confirmation

Between Nomination and Confirmation

Well, you have been nominated. That's progress, but you are now beginning another potentially long waiting period. This is also a very sensitive period in which your visibility should be very limited. From our interviews and research, we gained five insights into this time period:
- **Insight 9:** Be prepared for another (long) wait
- **Insight 10:** Mum is the word
- **Insight 11:** Spend time talking to your predecessors
- **Insight 12:** Spend time seeking out information
- **Insight 13:** Begin putting together your team (but be patient)

Insight 9: Be Prepared for Another (Long) Wait

Be warned!!! This can be a lengthy process. Our interviewees experienced wait times ranging from eight to 358 days, with three months being the average. A study of all Obama Administration nominees found that the average length of time between nomination and confirmation from 2009 to 2014 was 127 days, higher than the length of time for our interviewees (Samuelson). If you are lucky (or if there is a crisis in your organization needing the attention of a new appointee), your confirmation might be expedited. More likely, however, it will be a frustrating, slow wait.

Erica Groshen, Commissioner, Bureau of Labor Statistics, Department of Labor, had a long wait for her appointment. At the time of her nomination, she was a vice president in the Research and Statistics Group at the Federal Reserve Bank of New York. After her nomination in mid-February 2012, Groshen recalls, "I started spending my time finishing up my work at the Federal Reserve. I was put on 'garden leave,' which removed me from day to day activity. In July 2012, I was told that my nomination would be held up until after the presidential election in November. So I went back to work, doing some short-term projects…I was prepared for the possibility of a delay, and fortunately, I knew that if it ultimately did not work out, I could stay at the Federal Reserve. I focused on getting my work and home in order. I also spent time considering my living options and preparing a budget for Washington." Groshen was confirmed in January 2013, nearly 11 months after her nomination.

Gayle E. Smith had a similar long wait. Smith, a former national security aide to President Obama, was nominated in April 2015 to serve as administrator of the United States Agency for International Development. The previous administrator, Rajiv Shah, had left the position in February 2015. *The New York Times* reported, "Despite bipartisan support for Ms. Smith in the Senate, her confirmation has been tied up in a partisan fight over nominations. A Senate committee approved her by a voice vote on July 29 with no objections" (Nixon 2015). The full Senate vote was held up by one senator who said that he would object to any nominees for State Department posts because of his opposition to the nuclear deal with Iran. On November 30, a vote was finally held on the Senate floor. Ms. Smith was confirmed 79-7, seven months after her nomination.

Unlike Groshen and Smith, Terry Garcia's experience did not end as well. In May 2011, Garcia was nominated to be deputy secretary of Commerce, replacing Dennis Hightower. When nominated, Garcia was an executive vice president at the National Geographic Society. His nomination, along with several other Department of Commerce nominations, was held up by the Senate in order to put pressure on the White House to send three free trade agreements to Congress for approval. In October 2011, Garcia was reported to have become frustrated with the continued delay and asked that his nomination be withdrawn. An Administration official told Reuters, "He has been held up for no specific objection to him, his qualifications, or background. We've had this happen with a lot of our nominees, where there's an objection raised that has nothing to do with their qualifications" (Palmer 2011).

Insight 10: Mum Is the Word

Groshen summed up this period well. She recalls, "I was told what *not* to do. I was basically told to avoid doing anything public and not to talk to anyone."

The Groshen experience was typical for those interviewed for the project. All agreed that this was a difficult time period. Prior to setting a date for a confirmation hearing, there is likely to be little interaction between you and the department. Federal regulations also prohibit you from having office space in your new department or agency prior to your confirmation (the exception is if you receive another type of appointment, such as a special assistant, prior to your confirmation, which would then allow you to have space in a federal building).

Sloan Gibson, Deputy Secretary, Department of Veterans Affairs, describes his experience, "The time between nomination and confirmation was frustrating. Department officials could not speak to me and I was not getting information from the department. In this period, I did everything I could to prepare myself for the job. When we started getting ready for the confirmation hearing, I (finally) met with people in the department."

Insight 11: Spend Time Talking to Your Predecessors

David Stevens, former Assistant Secretary for Housing, and Commissioner, Federal Housing Administration, Department of Housing and Urban Development, did his homework for the new position on weekends while still working at his prior position. "I would spend weekends with binders to learn more about the department. I would also make phone calls on weekends to talk with people about the position. These phone calls were very helpful to me. You need to use your pre-confirmation time wisely. You should talk to previous incumbents and find out about their experience. I used the time to become as knowledgeable on issues as possible and find as many resources—both people and written materials—as I could."

Nearly all of those interviewed spent time talking with their predecessors. Many strongly advised seeking out predecessors from all previous administrations, regardless of party affiliation. Leon Rodriguez, Director of U.S. Citizenship and Immigration Services, Department of Homeland Security, recalls, "Regarding predecessors, I talked to Ali Mayorkas (my immediate predecessor) and two Bush (Republican) Administration appointees to this job. Ali gave me a fresh perspective on the agency. I had been an enforcement guy. I found my conversations with the Bush Administration appointees helpful. They told me that on a certain level, this agency is a factory—it's a huge organization with a huge amount of output. Part of the director's job is to make sure it works. While it does enforcement and legal affairs, it was a more complicated agency than just enforcement."

We also found agreement on both sides of the Atlantic that an important part of preparing for a new executive position in government is talking to your predecessor. Michael Roth, Minister of State for Europe at the German Federal Foreign Office tells us, "After I had been appointed, I contacted my predecessor. He belongs to another party, but I knew him well and we had always been on good terms. I asked him what to expect and what the pitfalls were."

Insight 12: Spend Time Seeking Out Information

Today, it is much easier to obtain information about your new agency than in the "old days." While you will ultimately receive briefing books in advance of your confirmation hearings, you will be "on your own" in the immediate days after your nomination.

"I have been confirmed twice for presidential appointments," recalls Kathryn Sullivan, former Assistant Secretary of Commerce for Environmental Observation and Prediction, and Deputy Administrator, National Oceanic and Atmospheric Administration (NOAA). "The confirmation process was similar in both instances, but my pre-confirmation preparations were very different. Prior to my first appointment, my parent agency detailed me to the office of the National Oceanic and Atmospheric Administration Administrator. The projects I took on for former Administrator John Knauss served as a great introduction to NOAA programs and issues."

"The second time (2010)," says Sullivan, "I relied on the Internet for my preparatory research. The variety and volume of materials available online—budgets, program evaluations, independent review reports, and more—allowed me to become quite familiar with NOAA's current operations and challenges."

The political executives we interviewed carefully reviewed Government Accountability Office reports, congressional testimony, speeches by former leaders, and comments by political leaders, regardless of party affiliation. Because of their prior research, they needed less time getting up to speed during their initial time on the job and had more time to spend on executing their agenda.

In addition to talking to predecessors, it is also helpful to seek out experts in your professional community to get their input into your new position. Peter Appel, former Administrator, Research and Innovative Technology Administration, Department of Transportation, recalls his experience: "I had been in the transportation business for 20 years, so I reached out to the 'wise' people in the profession to get their perspectives. I also talked to congressional staff."

Insight 13: Begin Putting Together Your Team (but Be Patient)

One of your early major responsibilities will be putting together your team. Although you will have a career staff in place, it may take a while to get your political team in place. Mark Rosekind, Administrator, National Highway Traffic Safety Administration (NHTSA), Department of Transportation, says, "Putting together my leadership team has been challenging, but we are steadily making progress. Important positions within the agency remain vacant, so we are working hard to recruit talented individuals to fill these critical roles and bring new perspectives to NHTSA. The DOT Office of the Secretary has been very supportive and even assembled a transition team to help after my confirmation. This team has been very helpful, and the next step is to bring in a strong leadership team that will remain with the agency for the long haul." The Rosekind experience is not unusual.

There are exceptions, however, to the slow pace of putting together your team. One success story of putting together a team was described by John Berry, former Director, Office of Personnel Management (OPM). Berry recalls, "I wanted to convey to the agency that we were ready to go. I wanted all my team in place on the same day that I started. I worked with the White House in getting my team cleared. We were all sworn in on the same day—my general counsel, director of congressional and legislative affairs, chief of staff, and the other key members of my team. This is the only time that the entire team has been sworn in on the same day. We wanted to get the team in place and get started." Berry and his team began work at OPM in April 2009.

Putting together an effective team that can work together will be crucial to your success. Most political executives fully understand the importance of their team. Putting together his team is described well by David J. Skorton, Secretary of the Smithsonian, who spent his first months putting together a team to work with him. He recalls, "Here's the secret: I can't do it all myself. I have really smart people; the team is really fantastic. The trick is to listen and not assume that because I have this big title I know more" (McGlone 2015a).

A key selling point in recruiting individuals to join your team is the mission of your organization. TJ Kennedy, former Acting General Manager, FirstNet, Department of Commerce, had the unique experience of recruiting an entire leadership team from scratch for a new organization. FirstNet was created by Congress to build, deploy, and operate the nationwide public safety broadband network. He recalls, "Three of us started in July 2013. We borrowed office space downtown in a Department of Commerce building. We first had to fill our C-suite positions and we had to get key staff to begin the acquisition planning process. Our main selling point in recruiting our team was our mission that will result in saved lives as we provide important tools to public safety personnel across the nation."

This mission of the organization was a primary factor in recruiting Russell Deyo to serve as under secretary for management in the Department of Homeland Security (DHS). In explaining his reasons for coming out of retirement to serve in DHS, Deyo told *The Washington Post,* "I don't have an agenda. This is not a stepping stone to anything. I'm here because of the secretary (Jeh Johnson), and I'm here because of the mission" (Markon).

Staffing to Meet Two Key Challenges

There are two "givens" in Washington which should be noted by all new political executives:

- **Congress will be a challenge.** In reflecting on his experience with Congress, Tim Geithner, former Secretary of the Treasury, writes, "Dealing with Congress, to put it mildly, did not feel like a careful, deliberative journey in search of the best public policy" (Geithner 2014). Ben Bernanke, former Chair, Federal Reserve System, adds, "It was inevitable that they (members of Congress) would ask questions for all sorts of purposes, but rarely because they were curious about the answer" (Bernanke 2015).
- **The media will be a challenge.** In reflecting on the differences in government from her most recent tenure, as contrasted with her previous tenure, Margaret Hamburg, former Commissioner, Food and Drug Administration, Department of Health and Human Services, reflects, "Government in general has changed dramatically, number one, because of the influence of the 24-hour news cycle" (Rubin 2015).

A good working relationship with both Congress and the media will be crucial to your success as a political executive. So be sure you put together top-notch press and legislative affairs offices.

Chapter Five

Arriving

Chapter 5

Arriving

You have now been confirmed and it is time to get started. Based on our interviews and research, we gained five insights into this time period:
- **Insight 14:** Have your bags packed, ready to go
- **Insight 15:** Don't expect the red carpet
- **Insight 16:** Beware of (too many) briefings
- **Insight 17:** Meet with career staff
- **Insight 18:** Listen
- **Insight 19:** Determine your time frame

Insight 14: Have Your Bags Packed, Ready to Go

While sometimes the United States Senate will have a clear schedule for confirming political appointees, more frequently they will not and prospective nominees will be caught by surprise at the date of confirmation. Confirmation votes often happen prior to the Senate going on a recess. Several of our interviewees were caught by surprise by their confirmation—after usually having waited for several months for the confirmation.

David Kappos, former Under Secretary of Commerce for Intellectual Property, and Director, United States Patent and Trademark Office (USPTO), Department of Commerce, recalls his experience. "The whole confirmation process places heavy demands on political appointees," recalls Kappos. "I was confirmed at 11:00 a.m. on a Friday and I was supposed to start work on the following Monday. I had to leave my family on short notice. There was no time to plan on where to stay. But I managed to get to D.C., find a hotel, and start on that Tuesday."

Richard Newell, former Administrator, U.S. Energy Information Administration, Department of Energy, had a similar experience. "My first day was on a Monday morning after I was confirmed on a Friday," recalls Newell. "I had already planned to drive up since I knew my confirmation was coming."

While many of those we interviewed arrived on the next working day or the following week after their confirmation, there were some who were delayed in arriving due to the bureaucracy in the organization they had been confirmed to lead. One appointee recalled, "I got confirmed on a Thursday. I thought I could show up on Friday and get started. But I could not get started until the following Monday since it did not fit the schedule of the Office of the Secretary. I wanted the weekend to come in and organize my office."

Insight 15: Don't Expect the Red Carpet

Arriving at the new office often brings surprises. Some political appointees might expect to have the red carpet rolled out for their arrival. Former Chair of the Consumer Product Safety Commission Inez Tenenbaum's experience was different. "The physical office space was a real mess," recalls Tenenbaum. "The walls had not been painted. I found old furniture in my office that needed replacing. The building itself was run down. It was a pretty dreary place. We had very few supplies, and we also had no business cards or stationery. At the start, I just had one staff member who I brought with me from South Carolina. We have since improved the physical look of the building and created standard operating procedures."

Rhea Suh, former Assistant Secretary for Policy, Management and Budget, in the Department of the Interior, had a similar experience. She recalls, "During my interview process for the job, I visited the building and was struck by how old the building was. It was really worse for wear. And my new position was responsible for the building. I felt like the building needed a fresh coat of paint. I wanted to make the building more inviting."

In addition to reacting to your new physical space, you will usually be arriving alone without any additional political executive colleagues. Allison Hickey, former Under Secretary for Benefits, Department of Veterans Affairs, recalls her experience: "I was obviously not a stranger [to] government. I knew the government, its culture, and rules. I had spent 27 years in the military and 17 years in the Pentagon. Part of my first day felt very normal, but there were differences. I came in without knowing anybody—not a single soul. This is different from the military where you know a lot of people. I had to learn a new set of languages and meet new people."

John Porcari, former Department of Transportation (DOT) Deputy Secretary, had a similar experience. He recalls, "I felt like an outsider. I had only been in the building twice before. I had never been invited in the building by the prior administration. I was familiar with the organization of DOT since the Maryland Department of Transportation (which I headed) was set up the same way DOT is. We had highways, airports, and ports in Maryland. But I found DOT to be somewhat alien and very different. I felt I was largely on my own in the beginning. I knew some people in the department."

Insight 16: Beware of (Too Many) Briefings

Marcia McNutt, former Director, U.S. Geological Survey, Department of the Interior, recalled that her initial days were spent receiving briefings. "I was overtaken by briefings in the first days and weeks," says McNutt. "My days were taken up by briefings. I had just gotten sworn in when I started to get briefings. There were lots of things that the agency wanted me to know about, and there were conferences and Congressional testimony coming up on a variety of topics. But I felt that the agendas were being managed and I felt that I had other things to do. The person who controls the agenda controls the outcome of the meeting."

"My time was being chunked up into 15-minute components. I think the intent was good—the agency wanted to tell me as much as they could in a short amount of time. But I needed to have more time for myself so that I could figure out what needed to be done. I had to decide what I should focus on."

The challenge of first weeks in office and sorting out the information being given to you is captured very well by Eric Lucas, General Secretary of the Ministry of Justice in France. Lucas recalls, "The first week everything is unfamiliar. You explore and try to identify who makes decisions and what decisions are being made. It takes a few months to come to understand the organization and to see weaknesses because we are dependent on what people can tell us and what they are concealing or do not perceive."

"After three months I understood how the ministry worked, but then the difficulty concerned the core details of the legal and penitentiary professions. Everyone here is a magistrate and they all know each other. It's not easy to penetrate this network and decipher its codes. We have to trust what people tell us."

Insight 17: Meet with Career Staff

Career Staff at Headquarters

Many of our interviewees immediately met with their career staff after their arrival. Kappos held a staff meeting during his first morning on the job. "At 11 a.m. on Tuesday, I conducted my first staff meeting," says Kappos. "Everybody was a bit nervous about the new guy on board. I knew the issues facing the USPTO, so I wanted to get off to a fast start. I know you only have a certain period of time in these jobs so I didn't want to waste a single day."

Mary Wakefield, former Administrator, Health Resources and Services Administration, Department of Health and Human Services, reached out to the entire organization. She recalls, "The first day I was here, there was a lot of excitement. People were both excited and apprehensive. On the day I arrived, I went though the entire agency—1,600 people. We have 10 divisions on 10 floors. I was excited about the privilege of holding office and the opportunity to work with great people. I spoke to each of the divisions that ranged in size from 70 to 200 people. I wanted face time with each office. I wanted them to see me and I wanted to see them…I wanted to affirm the value of the agency and public service. I did not want to be just somebody who resided on the 14th floor…I told them I valued their expertise and viewed them as members of our team. It was a good start. I wanted them to know who I am."

An interesting finding from our interviews was the eagerness of career civil servants to meet with and hear directly from the new political appointee. Suh recalls, "An important thing to know is that my position had been vacant for most of the previous two years (dating back to the prior administration)...I think this created a higher anxiety from civil servants than usual. Some were anxious with eagerness to finally have a new leader in place. Others viewed my arrival with some trepidation. Some people were eager for new leadership while others were not. I felt I had to meet people and earn their respect. They wanted to know what I wanted to do."

Kathryn Sullivan, former Assistant Secretary of Commerce for Environmental Observation and Prediction, and Deputy Administrator, National Oceanic and Atmospheric Administration, was also eager to meet with her staff. She recalls, "I wanted to hit the ground running and become familiar with our operations and people as quickly as possible. I had countless briefings and made a point of getting out to meet with people. I had been appointed to a newly created position and felt it was important for our people to get to know me."

It is especially important to communicate to staff if there are potential budget cuts (or other problematic issues) on the horizon that are likely to be alarming. Erica Groshen, Commissioner, Bureau of Labor Statistics, Department of Labor, recalls, "I wanted to get out in front of employees as soon as possible. We had six town hall meetings as part of what I called my 'listening tour.' I wanted to talk to them about budget cuts, to introduce myself and hear what was on their minds."

Career Staff in the Field

In addition to meeting with career staff whom they would be working with daily at headquarters, many of our interviewees emphasized the importance of meeting those in the field as well. Given the vast array of field offices, Kathleen Merrigan, former Deputy Secretary, Department of Agriculture (USDA), made visits with field staff a priority. "I try and visit our field offices whenever I travel. Many employees in our county offices had never had people from Washington visit, not just in this administration, but some tell me not in the 35 years that they have worked for USDA. Employees come to these meetings expecting a big speech, but after five minutes of remarks, I turn to questions and assure them that they can be frank and that everything is on the table."

Getting out to the field to meet employees was a common experience nearly all of our interviewees described, including those in Europe. Many tell us that was one of the first activities they had undertaken after their appointment. Jürgen Gehb, Spokesman of the Board of the German Institute for Federal Real Estate, described his experience: "I tried to make myself known within the organization. We have offices scattered all over Germany—from Freiburg in the south to Rostock in the north, and from Aachen in the west to Frankfurt an der Oder in the east. The structure is a bit like a spider web. The head office is located in Bonn. Then there are nine directorates and around another 120 smaller units. I wanted to find out what kind of people worked for the Institute for Federal Real Estate and how the organization ticks. That was the part of my new role I enjoyed most because here my duty and my inclination coincided. I enjoy the exchange with our employees as well as with our customers."

In the United States, Michael Huerta, Administrator, Federal Aviation Administration (FAA), Department of Transportation, tells us, "Whenever I am out of town, I take time to visit two or three FAA facilities. I don't just visit control towers—that is just too easy. I meet with our operating offices and talk to employees. I don't deliver talking points anymore. I just talk to them and answer questions. Many FAA employees are not used to seeing people from headquarters, including the administrator."

Dennis Hightower, former Deputy Secretary, Department of Commerce, spent time during his first months in the department on the road. "I spent time out in the field where the work gets done," recalls Hightower. "I wanted to meet the Commerce employees, and observe firsthand how they performed their work. I used different forums to talk with employees. I would ask a lot of questions. I used this time to think strategically about the Department."

Hickey visited employees in Veterans Benefits Administration (VBA) regional offices during her first several months in office. "I wanted to learn the VBA business and understand the process," says Hickey. "I wanted to see what they were doing and experience firsthand our claims processes and challenges. I did this for all lines of business. I wanted to understand our businesses."

Insight 18: Listen

Listening Inside Your Organization

Another theme from our interviews was the need to listen and learn about the new organization and how it operates. Abigail Ross Hopper, Director, Bureau of Ocean Energy Management, Department of the Interior, recalls, "I started on January 5, 2015, and kept quiet for a month. I did not see any need to talk up during my first month. I wanted to see how things operated in the department. I went to plenty of meetings in my early days."

David J. Skorton, Secretary of the Smithsonian, followed a similar strategy. Shortly after starting his new position, Skorton told *The Washington Post*, "For the first quarter, the first 100 days, to use a cliché, I will be listening. I think it is important for me to be out and hear what people have to say ... I've been visiting different places without my handlers, asking people what they think. It's a different experience. I'm going to try to keep doing that. You can get more information when you get out of office than if you stay in" (McGlone 2015b).

Allison M. Macfarlane, former Chair of the Nuclear Regulatory Commission, also emphasized listening. She recalls, "I knew I had to walk the walk. I had to be a good listener. I wanted to show that staff that I was concerned and that I understood the issues. I had an open door policy. I walked around a lot. I found a lot of opportunities to communicate. I also met with the commissioners on a weekly basis. I was able to establish collegial working relationships with my fellow commissioners." It should be noted that Macfarlane succeeded a commissioner, Gregory Jaczko, who had been forced to resign due to his poor relationship with his fellow commissioners and his controversial management style within the agency. All four commissioners (two Democrats and two Republicans) had written a letter to the White House complaining about Jaczko's management practices. It was thus essential for Macfarlane to reestablish a good working relationship with commissioners, as well as agency staff (Broder and Wald 2011).

The need to observe and listen is even more crucial when one arrives during the second year of an administration, or the second term, when processes and procedures are already in place. Sloan Gibson, Deputy Secretary, Department of Veterans Affairs, arrived in February 2014, one year after the start of the second term. He recalls, "I was determined to come in the door to understand and listen. I came to work for a secretary (Eric Shineski) who had been running the place for five years. I was trying to absorb as much information as I could as fast as I could. I wanted to get my oar in the water."

Listening Outside Your Organization

In addition to meeting with internal staff, many of those interviewed described wanting to meet with key stakeholders outside of the department. Merrigan recalls, "Knowing that everybody would want to come in and make a case for priorities for the new administration, I accepted all meeting requests for the first three months. This prevented a logjam of requests and allowed me to establish relationships with important constituent leaders."

Insight 19: Determine Your Time Frame

As described in this section, your early days will go quickly. You will be busy receiving briefings (and more briefings), meeting with your career staff, and meeting with stakeholders outside your organization. There will probably be some immediate fires to put out.

While this is a delicate subject, it is important to have a sense of your own time frame. Seldom at the start of an administration will it ask appointees to commit to serving for a specific period of time. If an appointment is made during the second half of the first term, an appointee may be asked to serve for the remainder of the first term (or the remainder of the second term if appointed halfway through the second term).

In the federal government, all appointees know the time cycle of an administration. During the first term, it is known that the president will be up for reelection in four years (unless he or she does not run for a second term). If an appointee joins the administration during the summer of the first term (as many of our interviewees did), that gives him or her approximately three years to get something done prior to the fall presidential campaign. Because it is difficult to see into the future, political appointees do not know whether they will have a chance to serve during a second presidential term, which would give them the opportunity to solidify accomplishments made in the first term.

The likelihood of a relatively short tenure (perhaps two to three years) is often first and foremost on the mind of a new political appointee. Based on his previous experience in government, Seth Harris, former Deputy Secretary, Department of Labor, says, "I realize how short the time you have in government really is when you're a political appointee. The challenge is whether you are going to leave 'footprints in concrete' or 'footprints in the snow.' There are so many things that can be undone after you leave or an administration changes. This time around, I came to a better understanding of how to succeed here."

Chapter Six

Starting

Starting

Now the hard part begins. The challenge of getting started in your early months cannot be underestimated. "It's the old story about finding your parking spot," recalls Marcia McNutt, former Director, U.S. Geological Survey (USGS), Department of the Interior. "I came to USGS from an institute where we had 230 employees, to an organization with nearly 9,000 employees. You can get lost in the building. It must have been designed by the CIA. You need friends to find your way around here."

Leon Rodriguez, Director, U.S. Citizenship and Immigration Services, Department of Homeland Security, described his experience as jumping into deep water. Reflecting on getting started, Michael Roth, Minister of State for Europe at the German Federal Foreign Office, recalls, "It was like taking a crash course! It was learning by doing: getting to know colleagues, structures, developing a work routine because it was a bit different to the kind of work I'd done before. As a member of parliament I was my own boss, whereas now as a minister of state I'm part of a more complex organization."

Kathleen Merrigan, former Deputy Secretary, Department of Agriculture, had an experience similar to Roth's. She recalls, "Even though I have worked in agriculture policy for the better part of my career, it still took me a while to gain my footing. A bureaucracy this vast and complex is tough to manage. You have to know how to delegate, how to establish trust with your career managers, and then quickly decide where to leave your fingerprints. As a political appointee, time is not on my side…"

Like Merrigan, Pamela Hyde, former Administrator, Substance Abuse and Mental Health Services Administration (SAMHSA), Department of Health and Human Services, was surprised at how much she did not know. Hyde recalls, "I did not know how many small grants programs we had at SAMHSA. I've been at all levels of government, but I still didn't have any idea of the complexity and size of the federal government."

Based on our interviews and research, we gained three insights into this time period:
- **Insight 20:** Deal with immediate problems and find out existing agency commitments
- **Insight 21:** Assess your organization
- **Insight 22:** Decide how many items on which to focus and the pace of change

Insight 20: Deal with Immediate Problems and Find Out Existing Agency Commitments

You will likely come into office facing some immediate fires and unfinished business from the prior administration. You will also have to determine if there is an agenda or commitments already on the table for you to oversee or whether

> ### The 90-Day Mark
>
> Several of the political executives we interviewed commented on feeling more comfortable after about three months in office. Former Department of Transportation Deputy Secretary John Porcari recalls, "After 90 days, I began to know 'what I didn't know' and 'what I needed to know.' The beginning days were like flying a plane. You have to be constantly scanning and looking over the horizon from the cockpit." Leon Rodriguez, Director, U.S. Citizenship and Immigration Services, Department of Homeland Security, had a similar experience: "There was a point toward the end of my first three months when I felt I 'owned' all the challenges and issues facing the agency."

there is flexibility on setting the agenda. It is important to understand what your organization is already committed to prior to undertaking a new set of activities or priorities.

But first, you must deal with immediate issues facing your organization. Erica Groshen, Commissioner, Bureau of Labor Statistics, Department of Labor, recalls, "My first 24 hours were my hardest. I had to choose to eliminate three programs due to the FY 2013 sequestration. I discussed with the staff why it made sense to cut these three programs. I had to get up to speed quickly and fully understand the reasoning behind this plan before signing my name to it. Eliminating these programs, valuable though they were, allowed us to continue producing our remaining reports without damaging their quality. In addition, since these cuts did not reduce costs enough immediately, we froze hiring, postponed investments and delayed training for employees over the year. No day since then has been so hard."

Many of those we interviewed during the first year of the Obama Administration (those arriving either during summer 2009 or fall 2009) found that an agenda and commitments were already in place. In February 2009, Congress passed the American Recovery and Reinvestment Act (the Recovery Act); it had been developed by Obama's transition team during the November to January transition and sent to Congress shortly after inauguration. Many agencies were tasked with implementing the Recovery Act and getting the money "out" to the states and other recipients.

Implementing the Recovery Act is described well by Jonathan Adelstein, former Administrator, Rural Utilities Service (RUS), Department of Agriculture. "By the time I was confirmed by the Senate in the summer, much of the work on setting up the Recovery Act's Broadband Initiatives Program had been completed with oversight from the secretary's office and the White House," remembers Adelstein. "So I didn't have a role in the design of the first round of the program. I had to work with what I found. I gave a speech to the agency within a week of my arrival… I let the staff know that I supported their mission."

Political executives also frequently arrive after a mandate has been handed down by the Office of Management and Budget (OMB) to undertake a specific set of activities. The late Brad Huther recalls his arrival at the Department of Housing and Urban Development (HUD) as Chief Financial Officer: "In 2013, before my arrival, OMB had mandated the drastic move that HUD go to shared services. We had to redirect everything to shared services. We started shared services in October 2014. It was a whole new process and we were the first cabinet department to do it. We had to develop a plan to do this and we had to restructure our team and develop a new schedule. We had to build political support for this change within the department and had to report to OMB once a week on our progress. We also had to replace one of our contractors on the project, which took time and effort, but we got it done."

Insight 21: Assess Your Organization

Political executives face their initial management challenge when they arrive at the office on their first day. They must decide how quickly they want to move on assessing their organization. David Kappos, former Director, United States Patent and Trademark Office (USPTO), Department of Commerce, wanted to meet quickly with his staff so that each could begin to assess one another. "I wanted to get a running start and hit the ground running, but I didn't want to jump out of the chopper shooting."

Nearly all of the political executives interviewed wisely avoided the tendency to "jump out of the chopper shooting." David Stevens, former Commissioner of the Federal Housing Administration (FHA), Department of Housing and Urban Development, describes his deliberative pace in assessing his organization. Stevens recalls, "I spent my first days at FHA assessing the organization. I would go out into the field and talk with our staff. We held large staff meetings and an offsite planning retreat. I wanted to better understand the major issues facing the department. I focused on what I thought I could accomplish and what would make a real difference."

What You Bring to the Table

There are clear advantages to having new political executives coming into government bringing new perspectives from the outside. James Runcie, Chief Operating Officer (COO), Office of Federal Student Aid (FSA), Department of Education, reflects, "I thought the agency did not compare well to the private sector in regard to customer service. I had come from the private sector. There was not much market or customer segmentation here. I thought the agency was not keeping up with changes in the outside world. Things are moving fast in the private sector, especially in areas like call centers. I also thought the agency was behind in social media."

During his initial assessment, Stevens says, "It became obvious to me that we needed to better manage risk. We needed a risk office and a chief risk officer. I felt FHA needed to go outside of the organization to recruit some top-notch deputy assistant secretaries. We needed to recruit people with experience in credit risk, credit policy, and lending." Unlike several of the executives profiled here, Stevens concluded during his assessment of the organization that reorganization was not needed. "I decided," recalls Stevens, "that I didn't want to reorganize. So I put my efforts into assessing the talent already in the organization."

Several of the political executives we interviewed launched an initiative to examine a specific set of activities within the organization. Often these review initiatives result in personnel changes. John Thompson, Director, United States Census Bureau, Department of Commerce, recalls, "When I got here, Census staff were all over the map about how to proceed in 2020. The staff had come up with several different designs. I needed to get the staff to understand a new way to manage the census. We could not simply use our existing methodology...We launched a 'rocket team' to evaluate our thinking on the 2020 Census. We needed a new approach. It took six months. In that time, I also put in a new leadership team for the Decennial Census."

Assessments of the organization are especially crucial when a political executive arrives to find the agency in a firestorm of negative publicity. David Strickland, former Administrator of the National Highway Traffic Safety Administration (NHTSA), Department of Transportation, found himself in that situation when he arrived in the midst of the furor over the Toyota automobile recall. "When I got here in January (2010), there had already been a significant amount of work in progress on Toyota," recounts Strickland. "There was much work underway, including a study by the National Academy of Sciences and a research initiative with the National Aeronautics and Space Administration. My first task was to determine whether NHTSA was broken. Some people were saying that we had a broken culture here. I decided that they were wrong and that NHTSA was not broken. That decision was a risk I had to take, but I believed it. It turns out that I was right. The final analysis showed that NHTSA had done a fantastic job on the Toyota recall."

In some cases, problems find the new political executive. Jonathan Adelstein, former Administrator, Rural Utilities Service (RUS), Department of Agriculture, recalls, "When I got here, I quickly found that we had a crisis in management regarding the information technology system we were using to accept applications for broadband projects. The process was in meltdown due to the unprecedented number of applications for loans and grants. RUS was working with another agency on application intake and it just wasn't working. It was a stressful situation in the beginning."

While you will not be surprised at finding problems, you should also not be surprised to find a well-running organization. Hyde recalls, "There had been a good acting administrator prior to my getting here. Things were running pretty smoothly. So it was not a case of coming in to clean up the agency. But being in good shape is both a blessing and a curse. The good news is that nothing is going wrong. The bad news is that it is harder to make change in an agency in which things are going well."

Insight 22: Decide How Many Items on Which to Focus and the Pace of Change

We were struck by the various approaches that the political executives we interviewed took to the decision as to how many issues on which they should focus. Margaret Hamburg, former Commissioner, Food and Drug Administration (FDA), Department of Health and Human Services, was advised by several former commissioners to just pick out a couple of issues and focus on those items. "Instead," Hamburg recalls, "I found that I had to focus on positioning FDA for the future. I wanted it to be as effective as it could be. This required a whole new level of engagement with the agency. I wanted to strengthen the quality of the work done here. The agency needed an advocate for itself. There was no beginning and end to the initiative of improving the agency. I felt that if we didn't address this issue, we would be losing critical ground. We needed to forge stronger working relationships with many groups. We have gone up in public approval of the agency."

Kappos reached a similar conclusion to Hamburg in response to the myriad challenges facing the United States Patent and Trademark Office. Kappos launched an aggressive campaign on many fronts, saying, "The job of leadership is to work on all the challenges. You need to do it all. There is no one single thing that you have to do; you have to do a hundred things. Change is the sum

---

**Some Guiding Principles from John Morton,
Former Director, United States Immigration and Customs
Enforcement, Department of Homeland Security**

"We have 20,000 people here. My previous experience did not prepare me to manage such a large operation. This is a different kettle of fish. But the principles I developed as a prosecutor have been helpful. I know you need to focus on the mission. You have to get it right on the substance. You don't need to yell or scream. You have to admit when you don't know something. You can only delve down every so often. You have to work to create space for the agency. It is a balancing act. You have to make decisions, but you can't spend all your time on 50 decisions. There are certain things that I would be good at but they aren't my job. I have to limit myself and know what is not my job. I cannot get down into the weeds."

of a lot of little things. I don't believe there is a magic bullet or a single fix. I believe it is about making day-by-day changes and continuously working toward improvement. I believe philosophically that you are never done. Change goes on forever."

Stevens selected a different path. Because of the financial crisis confronting the nation and HUD when he arrived at FHA, Stevens adopted a management strategy to focus on just a few major issues. "I've learned to just focus on two or three issues and give those my full attention," says Stevens. "That meant I gave other issues much less attention. On the other issues, I just needed to know enough to give people my go-ahead to keep them going. You really have a short time here and you have so much to get done, you have to focus on just a few things. I had to focus on a couple of things and dig in to get them done."

One of the factors in deciding how many items on which to focus is how many initiatives the agency staff can "absorb" in a short time span. Christoph Verenkotte, President of the German Federal Office of Administration, described this issue well: "I took on a lot of work at the start, launching a series of projects and tackling various topics—and everyone started complaining after about six months... After all, open communication isn't everything. You also have to make sure that your employees are not overwhelmed. Many quickly start to feel misunderstood with respect to the value attributed to their everyday work. When new projects come along, employees normally react by saying: 'But we already have enough to do anyway! Do they have no idea what we do every day, and now this ...' New projects are always viewed as being added on top of everything else, and this can become problematic if you don't keep a lid on it and explain the reasons behind it in more detail. This is something that I came to realize, but it is not always easy to respond to."

Mark Rosekind, Administrator, National Highway Traffic Safety Administration, Department of Transportation, described a similar experience: "The intensity and tempo are never-ending. But I am becoming more knowledgeable about all the tools we have available. There is no resting easy here ... There was one staff meeting early on where a lot of new ideas were developed and subsequent assignments were handed out. One staff member said after the meeting, 'Can we stop adding more to-dos to our agenda?'"

Deciding on the pace of change is especially important when a new political executive follows an executive who had made changes to a major initiative. In recalling his experience following William Taggart at FSA, James Runcie, current COO at FSA, recalls, "I had worked closely with Bill and had been part of his change agenda. I did not want to whiplash the agency on change. The agency has seen leaders come and go. They have seen it all. I wanted to stay the course and stay aligned with our five-year plan. I wanted to keep doing what we had been doing. I did not want to change what Bill had built just for change sake. I thought we needed a level of continuity. There was much relief throughout the organization when they found out there were not going to be any more changes."

It is clear that different strategies can work well in different situations. We observed, however, the key is consistent and ongoing focus. We saw this focus when we went back for our follow-up interviews. Most of our interviewees reported on their progress to date on a selected number of initiatives. In contrast, some executives presented a new list of items without discussing the status of their previous list. In some cases, a crisis or a new initiative from the cabinet secretary or the White House may have overridden the executive's initial list of priorities. But most important is continued focus—whether on a limited number of items or a larger number of items.

Chapter Seven

Deploying Management Levers

Deploying Management Levers

Your next challenge is to begin delivering high-level performance to the administration, your stakeholders, and the American public. In response to this challenge, we found that the political executives we interviewed spent much of their time in their first year on management-related issues; part of that was spent on deploying various management levers. In this section, we discuss the three levers that were mentioned most frequently in our interviews.

The need to focus on management and spend time on management-related issues and problems came as surprise to many who had come to Washington to spend time on policy issues. Sheila Bair, former Chairman of the Federal Deposit Insurance Corporation (FDIC), in her memoir, writes, "As it turned out, though I took the FDIC job because of my love for financial policy issues, I found that a substantial part of my time was spent dealing with management problems" (Bair).

Because of the major management challenges facing the Department of Energy, former Deputy Secretary Daniel Poneman recalls, "I've spent more time on management issues than I thought I would. Everything is a balance, so sometimes that meant I had less time to devote to interagency meetings or policy issues. But getting management right is essential to succeeding as a department."

Based on our interviews and research, we gained three insights related to the deployment of management levers in pursuit of high performance:

- **Insight 23**: Reorganize when needed (but not as your first option)
- **Insight 24**: Improve processes and technology
- **Insight 25**: Metrics can be a useful lever

Insight 23: Reorganize When Needed (But Not as Your First Option)

Reorganization, commonly called "moving around the boxes," is often the first impulse of a new leader eager to take charge and "shake up" the organization. We found, however, a range of opinions on reorganization from the political executives we interviewed. Some political executives embraced reorganization as a tool in which they could better align their organization for the future. Others were concerned that reorganizations were too politically contentious and too time-consuming, prompting the executives to caution against reorganization. It should be noted, however, that we found a wide range of initiatives called "reorganizations." Some were "full blown" reorganizations which realigned the organization, while others were minor reorganizations which fine-tuned the agency's organizational structure.

Realigning and clarifying the mission through reorganization. John Berry, former Director of the Office of Personnel Management (OPM), was one of the executives who concluded that his agency needed to be reorganized. Berry says, "It's the last thing I wanted to do, but I think we needed to do it. We needed to fix the agency and I owed it to the organization to do it. I just couldn't look away from our organizational problems."

Berry appointed a career OPM executive to lead the reorganization initiative. In reflecting on the reorganization, Berry says, "Looking at our old organization chart, you see how difficult it was to communicate what we do. It was self-evident that it needed fixing. We also needed to create some new organizational capability. I wanted the reorganization to be clean, simple, and fill our capability gaps."

Richard Newell, former Administrator, Energy Information Agency (EIA), Department of Energy, also concluded that a reorganization was necessary for his small organization. In describing his role pushing the reorganization, Newell says, "My role was critical. If I had not been driving the change, I don't think it would have happened. If you don't get involved, an initiative will just chug along. So we proceeded with the reorganization. We went from eight direct reports to me to four. We created a new structure that has four assistant administrators, each focused on a main EIA functional area—statistics, analysis, communications, and resources and technology management. It was a well-thought-out reorganization. It was not motivated to get rid of anybody. It was all about a better structure." Previously, the agency had been organized around the type of energy source, such as oil and gas; coal, nuclear, electric, and alternate fuels; and energy markets.

In contrast to some of the other appointees interviewed, David Stevens, Commissioner, Federal Housing Administration, Department of Housing and Urban Development, decided not to reorganize. Stevens concluded that a full-scale reorganization was not needed during his assessment of the organization. "I decided," recalls Stevens, "that I didn't want to reorganize. So I put my efforts into assessing the talent already in the organization. At Freddie Mac, I had spent too much time on reorganization rather than on dealing with other crucial issues. My time at Freddie Mac was very valuable to me. I worked on multiple issues there which turned out to be excellent training for this position."

The major reason presented for reorganizing was the need to better align the agency to its mission. Many of the political executives interviewed reported that they found their organization not aligned to meet their current mission and that this misalignment was often reflected in the agency's organizational structure. Patrick Gallagher, former Director, National Institute of Standards and Technology (NIST), and Under Secretary of Commerce for Standards and Technology, Department of Commerce, concluded that reorganization was necessary for his agency to achieve greater alignment between organizational units.

From Gallagher's perspective, the NIST reorganization was not an end in itself. Rather, it was a crucial element of his strategy to change NIST's culture and to strengthen the organization to survive the fast pace of change in the 21st century. "The reorganization was never just about organizational structure or who reports to whom. It wasn't about boxes," he says. "It was about getting the organization better aligned. We wanted to get the right people and align them in the new organization. Alignment was our larger goal. We needed to reset the agency."

Gallagher's management agenda was to move NIST away from an activity-based structure for the agency's laboratories, which were organized like a university. "In that structure, our managers acted much like chairs of academic departments," Gallagher recalls. "We wanted to move toward a mission approach." Many of the science-based political executives interviewed came to the conclusion that the academic orientation and "department-like" structure of their government agency was no longer appropriate to meet their needs in the 21st century.

Fine-tuning the organizational structure. Pamela Hyde, former Administrator of the Substance Abuse and Mental Health Services Administration (SAMHSA), Department of Health and Human Services, also concluded that a reorganization was necessary. She felt that she needed to fine-tune the organization to better accomplish its mission. Hyde recalls, "I found that policy was everyplace. We had some policy in the budget office. There were also policy people in the Office of the Administrator. The centers within SAMHSA were very siloed. Policy was very diffuse in the agency, so we created a new policy office. We have about 50 people all together ... We also moved grants management into finance, so that we had all the money functions in the same place. We still have activities spread out all over the agency. We have homeless programs in all three centers. We are not organized for the 21st century. We had to push through reorganization…It is still in process."

Jon Wellinghoff, former Chairman of the Federal Energy Regulatory Commission (FERC), came to a similar conclusion. He felt he needed to create two new offices within FERC to enable the agency to more effectively contribute to policy discussions in the future. Wellinghoff recalls, "I thought we needed to analyze new ideas. There were specific issues on which I wanted to work. I thought we needed a new policy office. We now have 11 offices, including a new Office of Energy Policy Innovation and an Office of Energy Infrastructure Security. In creating the Office of Energy Infrastructure Security, we wanted to have more expertise on the Interstate grid and want to mitigate threats, including cyber threats and physical threats. This has been an extremely successful office. It has helped us on rulemaking and we are now better prepared to work on cybersecurity and other infrastructure issues."

Insight 24: Improve Processes and Technology

As part of their focus on management related issues, many executives we interviewed found it necessary to examine the agency's internal operations and work processes. Seth Harris faced both people and process issues in his role as deputy secretary of labor. "We had to improve the business practices of the department," asserts Harris. Based on his previous experience in government, Harris says, "You have to change the processes and make it the new way of doing business. You need to implement repetitive processes. While it is difficult to do, you can do it. You can give people a new set of tools. You can start them using program evaluation and developing operating plans."

In reflecting on his experience, Harris says, "I've learned that you need to engage the civil service to change the DNA of the organization. You can get the department to start using new procedures which will be the way they do business in the future by building on and adapting existing procedures that they have used for years. Mixing the new with the old seemed to be a recipe for successful change. You have to get into the systems of government. You can change government, but it takes time."

In some cases, a political executive is hired specifically to improve the processes of the organization. Referring to his discussions with Secretary Shaun Donovan about his position as deputy secretary at the Department of Housing and Urban Development (HUD), Maurice Jones recalls, "It was clear that I was going to focus on operational excellence ... I have been focusing on human capital and financial processes. You can have the greatest, most innovative policies, but without execution, these policies can't succeed." Jones also notes his concern about the health of the organization. "I want to leave the department a better place. I would say the long term health of the organization is at risk ... We need to focus on people, processes, and priorities."

There are many examples of political executives focusing on improving processes. A backlog problem faced Allison Hickey, former Under Secretary for Benefits, Department of Veterans Affairs. Much of the growth in backlog was due to an increase in both the number of claims and complexity of the claims. In order to improve the process, the Veterans Benefits Administration (VBA) began to treat less complex claims differently than more complicated claims. VBA created "express lanes" for certain claims. "We are able to push these less complicated claims through at a faster pace," describes Hickey. "If we can do this, there will be less work on the front end. We can get less complicated claims through, which will then allow us to spend more time on tougher, more complicated claims. We are trying to manage our throughputs."

Former Administrator John Pistole, Transportation Security Administration, Department of Homeland Security, also put an emphasis on improving processes. After his arrival in June 2010, Pistole quickly came to the conclusion that his agency needed to change the way it was operating. "We had been using a one-size-fits-all approach," says Pistole. "But I knew it didn't have to be this way. As an FBI agent, I would get on a plane with special treatment. So I knew we were already treating people differently. I knew that there were many possibilities of doing things differently."

Coupled with improving processes, many political executives found they also needed to work on simultaneously improving their technology. Alejandro Mayorkas, former Director, U.S. Citizenship and Immigration Services (USCIS), Department of Homeland Security, recalls, "When I arrived, I found extraordinary workers with antiquated systems. I had a talented workforce and complex laws to administer with old systems in place. Our employees lacked access to the best and most updated support that industry has to offer. The agency receives seven million applications with antiquated resources. There is a great divide between people and technology."

Transparency and consistency between different offices were also issues Mayorkas faced. Mayorkas recalls, "A major criticism of us was the lack of consistency between offices. We had different policies in different offices...So different decisions were being made in different offices."

In clarifying the decision-making process at the Department of Education, former Deputy Secretary Anthony Miller worked to set clear expectations and explicit goals. "We developed an operational plan and shared it with staff throughout the department," says Miller. "It's important to let people know what is expected of their operating units. As leaders, we must be clearer and more transparent communicating performance expectations. This is basic management—setting forth your goals. We also started to link the planning process in the department with the budget process and get alignment. We have over 150 discretionary programs in the department, which were not well aligned."

Insight 25: Metrics Can Be a Useful Lever

In addition to improving processes, many political executives interviewed focused on metrics during their first year. David Kappos, former Director, United States Patent and Trademark Office (USPTO), says, "We understand our inputs and outputs at USPTO." In attacking the challenge of reducing the paperwork backlog, Kappos knew it was important to track the agency's progress—both to provide transparency to the public and to use it as a management tool inside the organization.

"The USPTO has a critical role to play in our economic recovery," Kappos told us in 2010. "That's why people really care about the backlog, which hinders innovation and economic growth. In response, we set specific targets. Our goal is to get the backlog under 700,000. We haven't been under that figure for many years. The goal is to get it down to a backlog of 325,000. That would be about 70 dockets per examiner, which is about right ... we set a 699,000 target for FY 2011. Getting under 700,000 would be a major accomplishment."

Kappos accomplished the goal in July 2011, when patents pending fell to 689,226. Since then, they have continued to fall and reached an all-time low in August 2012 when patents pending dipped to 623,168. Kappos created the PTO Dashboard, which is updated monthly on the agency's website to track progress on key performance indicators such as patents pending.

A similar situation faced Hickey during her first year at VBA. One of the items she quickly identified as a major challenge was the lack of metrics to measure success. Hickey faced a large inventory of claims and a backlog. On top of the existing claims inventory and backlog of regular claims she found upon arrival, there were new Agent Orange claims to settle. That required reallocating staff from processing other claims to complete the Agent Orange backlog. Over a two-year period, VBA received 260,000 claims from three new Agent Orange conditions, which required a surge of over 37 percent of VBA's workforce to adjudicate these claims.

Along with his focus on process issues discussed in Insight 24, such as the department's strategic planning process, former Deputy Secretary Harris concluded that the Department of Labor also needed new performance measures. "The department was measuring the wrong things," says Harris. "The measures were typically internal, and we were not measuring outcomes. The department had focused on outputs and process measures previously. We realized that measuring outcomes is incredibly hard, but absolutely essential."

Christopher Lu succeeded Harris as deputy secretary at the Department of Labor and continued much of the performance management system Harris had created. In reflecting on his experience setting targets, Lu comments, "We do set targets but it is a constant battle to make sure that you include some stretch goals. I tell our meeting participants that if we get to 90 percent of a goal, that is okay. I don't want people to be afraid of getting punished for missing a target. The goal is to get improvement."

For many executives, the key challenge is to decide on the metrics by which to assess their organization. Mayorkas recounts, "A key challenge is metrics. What is the appropriate metric for admitting people to the United States?" Traditionally, agencies have measured production in terms of how quickly they can complete a certain number of cases. Mayorkas says, "Given our responsibility to combat fraud and help safeguard our nation's security, a metric of production does not fairly address how we are executing on our mission."

We observed that political executives deploy metrics in the following ways:

- **Developing Metrics:** Political executives identified which metrics were linked to their organizational goals. USPTO, VBA, and USCIS identified completed applications as the key metric. The executives then developed specific target metrics for the organization to achieve in the completion of application reviews.
- **Using the Metrics:** Political executives regularly measured and received reports on the metric, relative to the target. When the organization fell short against the target, many political executives used this as an opportunity to examine why the organization had fallen short and what actions were needed to achieve the target.
- **Refining the Metrics:** Over time, the political executives changed or streamlined their metrics and targets to reflect enhanced organizational performance, or the fact that different management tools were needed.

Chapter Eight

Strengthening the Organization

Strengthening the Organization

Like many executives interviewed for our project, Mary Wakefield, former Administrator, Health Resources and Services Administration (HRSA), Department of Health and Human Services, came to Washington to work on policy. While Wakefield knew that she would be spending time working with HRSA's network of grantees and implementing the Affordable Care Act, she was surprised at the time required to work on strengthening the agency itself. Wakefield recalls, "I had to look at the infrastructure of our organization and how well it supported meeting our mission to improve access to quality health care. This involved carefully reviewing and adjusting our deployment of people and resources, from realigning the agency's organizational structure to investing in training and information technology. For example, too often we were still processing paperwork the old way and agency hiring was slow."

In reflecting on her accomplishments at HRSA, Wakefield says, "I think one of my major accomplishments is strengthening the organization. We now have a much stronger organization. I must admit that this took far more of my time than I anticipated, but meeting program and policy expectations is contingent on a high performing organization."

We found that many political executives strengthened their organizations in four ways:
- **Insight 26:** Enhance organizational capabilities
- **Insight 27:** Strengthen relationships inside and outside of the organization
- **Insight 28:** Increase credibility and visibility
- **Insight 29:** Position the organization for the future

Insight 26: Enhance Organizational Capabilities

After assessing their organization (Insight 21), many executives we interviewed moved to strengthening organizational capabilities. Just as they deployed management levers, political executives use the following approaches to enhancing organizational capabilities:
- Focus on personnel
- Change culture

Focus on personnel. A consistent theme from our interviews is the importance of getting the right people into the organization. While it has become a cliché in recent years, people are the organization's most important asset. According to the executives interviewed, this is especially true in government where "knowledge work" and "knowledge workers" are the norm. The federal government is widely credited with having the most educated workforce in the nation.

Daniel Poneman, former Deputy Secretary, Department of Energy, describes the importance of people in his organization. "The department is all about its people. It's a great organization that depends on a good esprit de corps," he explains. "The people I work with are glad to be here. They have engaging work."

Poneman devoted a significant amount of his time to people issues facing the department because of the importance of people to the successful accomplishment of the department's mission. "I've worked on ensuring that we have a process for getting good people into the department and then retaining them once they are hired and are here," says Poneman. He told *Government Executive* that hiring is only one part of the personnel challenge. "[Hiring] is just the front edge," he explains. "Our mission is evolving, and we need to continue to provide career paths that are exciting so we not only attract but retain talent" (Peters 2010).

Government science executives also emphasized the importance of people. "The Energy Information Administration (EIA) is all about its people—federal employees and contractors," says Richard Newell, former Administrator of EIA, Department of Energy. "It is a people organization. We have 370 federal employees with about 200 contractors. We need to keep them and attract new people. I'm pleased that people in our community are asking me about whether there are any new positions at EIA."

Patrick Gallagher, former Director, National Institute of Standards and Technology (NIST), Department of Commerce, was very clear about his deep commitment to the institution. "I want to create an environment conducive for our scientists," he says. "We have world-class scientists here. Our job is all about attracting people—hiring and then retaining them. Retaining people is always a challenge because they can make three or four times more money anywhere else, either in the academic community or [private] industry. Not only am I impressed that NIST has three Nobel Prize winners here, I'm more impressed that all three have stayed."

Margaret Hamburg, former Commissioner, Food and Drug Administration, Department of Health and Human Services, faced similar challenges to Gallagher's. She recalls, "We have all different kinds of scientists. We have lawyers and policy analysts. Their background makes all the difference. This agency is all about its people. This agency is not about grants and contracts. We study the law and examine consumer impact."

During his confirmation hearings, Arun Majumdar, former Director, Advanced Research Projects Agency-Energy (ARPA-E), Department of Energy, told Senate committee members that people were one of the five core values instrumental to ARPA-E. In describing his early days at ARPA-E, Majumdar tells us, "I started recruiting people. I wanted to get the right people. Putting together your team is critical. As a new agency with special hiring authorities, we had the flexibility to recruit outside of the civil service system. People didn't have to wait for six months to be hired. We have proved that good people will come here. We were able to get nearly all the people we wanted."

Because of his career-long interest in human resources, former Department of Veterans Affairs (VA) Deputy Secretary Scott Gould spent part of his first several months assessing the VA workforce. Gould concluded that the workforce needed strengthening. "I found a different style and culture in the department than I had anticipated," recalls Gould. "We had to keep asking people, 'What do you think?' and 'How will this serve veterans?' They often had a hard time answering. The career team was not as willing to question assumptions as I had anticipated. We concluded that we had to build the analytical and core skills of the organization, as well as create a culture of advocacy where they feel confident to speak their minds."

Nearly all those interviewed are very aware of the need to prepare for the forthcoming retirement wave among their civil servants. William Taggart, former Chief Operating Officer, Office of Federal Student Aid (FSA), Department of Education, tells us, "Nearly 20 percent of [our employees] will be eligible to retire in the next five years. We had only 975 people, with headcount falling, while our workloads were up 200 percent in some cases. It was clear that we needed to hire more staff to perform tasks that were deemed as 'inherently governmental.' We needed to hire the right people, with the right competencies, who knew how to work in a team-based environment."

Reflecting on his experience at the Department of Labor, Seth Harris, former Deputy Secretary, says, "Improving management in the department is a real challenge. We needed to improve the Senior Executive Service (SES) and develop an ever-stronger corps of SES members. We needed to define what it means to be an elite manager in the SES and what skills they need. We needed to do more skill development. I'm not just talking about training, I mean skill development. We also worked on individual performance measures and better SES evaluations."

Change culture. A key part of building organizational capacity is changing the culture of the organization. Rafael Borras, former Under Secretary for Management, Department of Homeland Security (DHS), describes this challenge. "There is the cultural part of my job which is less about policies," says Borras. "Culture and priorities interact with each other. We have many agencies (in DHS) that have their own history. We needed to get them to interact with each other and interact differently with each other. We want to change people's DNA, not just to change their minds."

Inez Tenenbaum, former Chairman of the Consumer Product Safety Commission, also recognized the importance of cultural change as part of building organizational capacity. Tenenbaum says, "We are trying to create a new culture here and get people to change the way they are doing business. We want to create a culture of excellence. We want to bring in new talent and get new people."

One of the many challenges facing Majumdar at ARPA-E was creating a positive culture for the new organization in which employees can flourish. Majumdar recalls, "I want innovation to be the DNA of ARPA-E. It is part of our core strategy. Once you get people here, you have to give them the freedom to solve problems. We want people who like being challenged. You have to create an atmosphere to allow them to have a real impact. You need to create a culture of openness and discussion. You don't want a top-down environment. What I have done is to create a culture which empowers people at ARPA-E, while also holding them accountable. I want people to succeed and want to create an environment for success. So the key elements to creating a culture are getting talent, creating an open dialogue, and allowing people to realize their potential."

Insight 27: Strengthen Relationships Inside and Outside of the Organization

We found that political executives spent a great deal of their time working to strengthen relationships with a variety of groups:
- Stakeholders
- Employees
- Congress
- White House and the Office of Management and Budget
- Their own departments

Strengthening stakeholder relationships. For the political executives interviewed, building relationships means reaching out to key stakeholders and partners both inside and outside of Washington, D.C. David Hinson, former National Director of the Minority Business Development Agency (MBDA), Department of Commerce, and Raymond Jefferson, former Assistant Secretary at the Veterans' Employment and Training Service (VETS), Department of Labor, adopted similar external strategies to achieve their missions.

"I spent a lot of time during my first year on the road building relationships," Hinson recalls. "You need to build good relationships with corporate America. Building these relationships is crucial." In describing his strategy for VETS, Jefferson says, "We want to create partnerships…to find employment opportunities for veterans."

Both Hinson and Jefferson developed working relationships with the Chamber of Commerce, among many other organizations, in support of their different missions: assisting minority businesses and assisting veterans with finding employment opportunities.

In the case of Michael Whitaker, Deputy Administrator, Federal Aviation Administration, Department of Transportation, one of his major responsibilities is working with the agency's private sector stakeholders. Whitaker tells us, "The agency has suffered from lack of engagement with the airline industry. When we do interact with them, lots of things get done. Some airlines feel disconnected. I view my job as bridging the two communities. We are always looking for opportunities for engagement. We have several important benchmarks coming up in 2020, so we need to work closely with the industry. We created a working group to look at some of the specific 2020 issues and are getting people to participate."

In looking back on her accomplishments after six years at the Food and Drug Administration, Margaret Hamburg says, "I feel I'm leaving a stronger, more engaged, and more effective agency. One of the hallmarks of my tenure has been an increasing emphasis on partnership with stakeholders. I came in at a time when there'd been a series of significant crises where the spotlight had been on FDA... There was a sense of being embattled with a constant negative drumbeat from the media, congressional criticism, oversight hearings, etc. When I came on board, there was a need to restore the trust and confidence in FDA, address important morale issues within the employee base, and really open up and engage. The only way to do our job well is to do it in a partnership with the public and the patients we serve, the industries we regulate, and importantly, the scientific community, to ensure we have the best possible science underlying our regulatory decision making" (Rubin 2015).

Special attention should be paid to a unique set of stakeholders: states and localities. "I've worked at the state, city, and county levels. States are now driving the health agenda of the nation," reflects Pamela Hyde, former Administrator, Substance Abuse and Mental Health Services Administration (SAMHSA), Department of Health and Human Services. "States are also now reorganizing by putting mental health and substance abuse programs together again. So our focus must now be on the states because of this particular time in history." As a consequence of Hyde's decision to place greater focus on the states, SAMHSA reorganized to create 10 regional administrators. "We are now organized around states," says Hyde. "We have regional groupings and technical centers. People in the states now know who to go to at the regional level. The White House is also very interested in states. Our challenge is how to bring states along."

Strengthening employee relationships. Building relationships also includes enhancing relationships with an organization's own employees. Taggart made employee engagement one of his top priorities. "Many of the staff worked at FSA an average of 18 years but did not feel valued by senior management," Taggart says. "I held several town hall meetings to get the employees' unfiltered feedback. They had a lot on their minds and were very vocal. That meant to me that they cared about the organization. It would have been much worse if I had been met with silence. It was essential for me to help the employees to feel better about the organization. I decided to get them involved in developing a new vision, mission, and core values for the organization. More than 200 employees participated in the process and helped to develop a new working relationship between the FSA employees and the COO."

Jonathan Adelstein, former Administrator, Rural Utilities Service, Department of Agriculture, also emphasized employee engagement. "I worked closely with the career staff here to make revisions in [procedures for] our second funding round. I wanted their buy-in and inspiration," he explains. "I wanted to know their ideas. We shared ideas and got different opinions on various options for round two. I believe in listening to staff. We had a very collegial relationship; it was not top-down. We had an ongoing dialogue."

The desire for openness with employees prompted Victor Mendez, former Administrator of the Federal Highway Administration, Department of

Transportation, to use a variety of outreach tools. "When I first got here, I drafted a message to employees," says Mendez. "We have done webinars and teleconferences with employees. We also have two annual meetings with all of our divisional managers and office managers. It is important for me to communicate with people and get out and mingle. I also follow up with employees via e-mail." The emphasis on communication was crucial to Mendez. "It may not be a great insight," says Mendez, "but I found communication to be very important. You need to repeat information to people and tell them what you are doing. You have to keep employees informed on the importance of issues and you have to work to develop your message to them."

Strengthening relationships with Congress. All those interviewed also recognize the importance of building relationships with members of Congress and their staffs. In explaining his strategy, Majumdar says, "I tell them what I do. I like to explain our agency in layman's terms. I try to make it easy for them to understand and talk to them in terms of impact and savings, while giving them the big picture. It's been a pleasant and enjoyable experience to work so closely with Congress. I'm from California and have never worked with Congress before. You need to spend time with them. They need to trust you. That takes time and you have to devote ongoing meetings to them."

Wakefield also recognized the importance of strengthening the agency's relationship with members of Congress. She recalls, "Some in Congress didn't seem to know much about the breadth and reach of HRSA's programs. I wanted to make sure that they knew about our agency and all of our programs and the extent to which we had activity underway in their state. I wanted them to be informed about HRSA's assets in their states and in service to their underserved and vulnerable populations. We needed to do a better job telling people, including Congress, what we do."

In addition to explaining their organizations to members of Congress and staff, there are also specific pieces of legislation on which political executives must work closely with members and their staff. In recalling his experience in working to get the Leahy-Smith America Invents Act passed, David Kappos, former Director of the United States Patent and Trademark Office, Department of Commerce, recalls, "I developed a close working collaborative relationship with two key members of Congress on the patent legislation. When we had an issue, we convened the right set of people to forge the necessary compromise…I encouraged constant engagement with congressional staff. We would invite them over for lunch and meet our staff. Leadership must encourage staff to engage with congressional staff. This is a relationship-based town. Investing in relationships will pay dividends. Everybody has to do it" (Kappos 2015).

Strengthening relationships with the White House and the Office of Management and Budget. Highly important to those interviewed is fostering relationships with the White House and the Office of Management and Budget (OMB). Former Office of Personnel Management Director John Berry says, "I wanted to develop a good relationship with OMB, which I have done. I work closely with OMB on all our initiatives. I've also engaged the White House on many initiatives, such as our activities on improving work life and veterans' hiring. We worked hard on building our relationship with the White House."

Working with the White House is indeed often a challenge. One of Deputy Secretary Sloan Gibson's initial assignments at the Department of Veterans Affairs was to improve the department's relationship with the White House, which had become strained due to the numerous performance problems at the department. Gibson recalls, "I was here for three days when I was sent to a meeting at the White House. I felt we had to change our attitude toward the White House. It has become an "us versus them" situation, but we had to be on the same side. I viewed the White House as an ally. I walked them through our issues. This behavior continues to this day."

The Office of Management and Budget is a formidable entity. In commenting on OMB, one former departmental deputy secretary says, "I was surprised by OMB. It's more difficult to get things done than I had anticipated. There was somewhat of a 'Mother may I?' attitude toward OMB within the department."

Daniel Ashe, Director, U.S. Fish and Wildlife Service (FWS), Department of the Interior, acknowledged the importance of working with oversight agencies both outside of his department as well as inside. Ashe reflects, "Most surprising to me is that as you move up in an organization, you would think you have fewer bosses. Instead, I now have many masters. This was a revelation to me which I had not expected. We work closely with the Office of Management and Budget. I work with the assistant secretary for fish and wildlife and parks who oversees both FWS and the National Park Service. As a result, there are more constraints than I had anticipated."

Strengthening relationships within your department. While it is easy to focus on external stakeholders, Congress, and the Office of Management and Budget, Linda Springer, former Director of the Office of Personnel Management, recommends that political executives also spend time with key colleagues in their own Department. She strongly recommends that political executives spend time getting to know their inspector general, chief financial officer, and staff in agency field offices (Springer 2013).

Insight 28: Increase Credibility and Visibility

Many of the executives we interviewed place great emphasis on enhancing the credibility and visibility of their agencies. Government agencies need to maintain a good reputation with Congress in order to receive their annual appropriations. But the leaders we interviewed also stressed internal reasons for enhancing an agency's credibility and visibility.

John Morton, former Director, United States Immigration and Customs

Enforcement, Department of Homeland Security, describes this challenge: "The agency needed a champion. We were doing fantastic work. The agency felt underappreciated. I felt that the men and women of this agency should get the recognition they deserved. It was the most misunderstood agency in government. I wanted to reshape the perception of the agency ... I wanted to promote and champion our investigative work. I want the agency to be recognized for its strong investigative arm. I wanted to tell people what we do."

Many executives were surprised by the low visibility of their agencies. As Under Secretary for Economic Affairs in the Department of Commerce, Rebecca Blank worked to boost visibility by finding opportunities in which economic analysis could contribute to policy making in the Administration. "We increased the visibility of the Economics and Statistics Administration in the White House," Blank says. "We are now getting more requests to do studies. The staff here is available to do this work and is enjoying getting involved in current issues and doing deep analysis. They like having new products and reports. These reports have generated requests from other parts of government to do similar studies."

Marcia McNutt, former Director of the U.S. Geological Survey (USGS), Department of the Interior, also determined that she would make it a priority to improve the credibility and visibility of her agency. She recalls, "I wanted to raise the status and prestige of the USGS. My impression is that organizations that are self-standing, like the National Science Foundation and the National Aeronautics and Space Administration, receive somewhat more attention than agencies like USGS, the National Institute of Standards and Technology, and the National Oceanic and Atmospheric Administration, which are within departments. Secretary Salazar does have an interest in USGS. In the past, USGS has often received little attention by departmental leadership. I want to increase the role of USGS in bringing science into decision-making."

It was felt by many interviewees, both in the United States and Europe, that an enhanced reputation might bring more resources to the organization, as well as improve working relationships with other government organizations. Jürgen Gehb, Spokesman of the Board of the German Institute for Federal Real Estate, describes his experience in Germany: "I felt that the purpose and significance of our work did not bear any relation to the recognition that the Institute for Federal Real Estate was receiving. We have a portfolio of 25,000 properties, some 490,000 hectares of land and 38,000 housing units, which makes us one of the largest owners of real estate in Germany...A major challenge is to improve the image of the Institute for Federal Real Estate. My responsibilities also include media and public relations. For example, not long after I took up office, I started organizing regular parliamentary evenings. My motto is: 'Don't just do good, talk about it!'"

R. Gil Kerlikowske expressed a similar concern from his vantage point as commissioner of the U.S. Customs and Border Protection (CBP) agency in the United States. He tells us, "I would like to improve the recognition of the agency within government. We don't get as much attention as we deserve. Before I got here, the head CBP was never invited to White House meetings. Since I knew the people at the White House, that changed when I arrived. I do understand the value of relationships."

Another way leaders and organizations can enhance credibility is an effective response to well-known external events. The U.S. Geological Survey (USGS) faced a series of natural disasters in a two-year period, including the Haiti earthquake in January 2010, the Iceland volcano in March 2010, and the Japanese earthquake in March 2011. USGS's response to the increased number of natural disasters had positive impacts inside the agency, as well as outside the organization. McNutt states, "I think we increased the stature of the agency, increased our visibility and our name recognition. We received much attention in 2010 and were on the front pages of many newspapers. We made a contribution in 2010. We were involved in responses to the earthquakes and volcanoes. It showed our diverse expertise in many areas. I think all the increased attention also helped inside the agency. It showed the relevance of the agency and it started people within the agency to think about things that we can do that they never imagined before."

Enhancing an organization's credibility is especially critical when an executive takes over an agency that has recently faced a crisis or a scandal. In taking on the position of director of the Minerals Management Service in the Department of the Interior in the aftermath of the Gulf Oil Spill in 2010, Michael Bromwich found a negative culture. He recalls, "The agency was suffering from years of negative publicity. There had been instances of corruption that had happened several years before ... There was massive media attention given to the agency and many negative stories ... We were the most heavily criticized agency in government when I started in June 2010, which did create a crisis mentality in the agency and in the Department of the Interior generally. We were being criticized in the media every day—every media outlet felt obliged to publish numerous critical pieces about the agency."

"Morale was as low as I've ever seen it in any organization," he continues. "There was a lot of tension in the agency, and a stream of negative commentary about it, including from inside the government. There was no end in sight to the negative publicity. I was very careful not to reinforce all this negative feedback by jumping on the bandwagon of criticism, but on the other hand I could not defend past acts of misconduct or lack of competence."

Hinson links improvements in the Department of Commerce's internal operations to its internal and external image. "I had to build credibility for the agency," Hinson says. "I wanted to show people what we were capable of doing. This required that we improve the skill sets of the agency. We had to make clear our expectations on training. I looked at everybody in the agency and decided what new capabilities we needed."

The Department of Homeland Security had been on the Government Accountability Office's High Risk List since 2003 when Borras arrived in 2010.

Hence, one of the major challenges facing Borras was enhancing the department's reputation and evaluations with its oversight organizations. Borras says, "Our efforts have helped enhance our conversations with the Government Accountability Office and other oversight groups. We come back with a plan now when we have a problem we are trying to solve, and a way to measure our progress."

Insight 29: Position the Organization for the Future

There was also agreement on the need for leaders to develop a clear vision for the future and position the agency to achieve that vision in the years ahead. Many of those interviewed emphasized that the career civil servants were primarily focused on operations; there were few, if any, leaders within the organization thinking about the future and what the organization might look like in five to 10 years. Erica Groshen, Commissioner of the Bureau of Labor Statistics, Department of Labor, tells us, "My job is to look over the horizon and think ahead. What will we be doing in the next 25 years and how do we position ourselves for it? During the last 10 years, no one really had talked explicitly about looking deep into the future."

Michael Huerta, Administrator, Federal Aviation Administration (FAA), Department of Transportation, came to the same conclusion as did Groshen. Huerta says, "This is a tactical place and not a strategic place. I spent time working on our strategic initiatives for the agency and thinking about the future of the organization."

In addition to working on the agency's strategic initiatives, Huerta also focused on improving the internal operations of the FAA and doing things differently. He recalls, "We had lots of internal discussions. Our senior staff saw the merits of doing things differently…Leading this discussion is an example of what I thought I could bring to the job—I could ask questions about what things we could do better. I told people that whether we are doing things differently would be one of our success factors."

In France, Jérôme Filippini, General Secretary of the Court of Auditors, also focused on the need for a long-term vision. He says, "Organizing your time is difficult, but it is priority. You have to take account of both the short- and long-term strategic vision. It is essential to carve out time for reflection and organization."

John Thompson, Director, United States Census Bureau, Department of Commerce, understood the role of chief executive based on his experience as a deputy in several organizations. He reflects, "In many of my positions, I had been a deputy to the leader of the organization. Those duties are completely different than those of the leaders. The CEO's job is to provide vision. They need to say where the organization should go and then make sure that the organization is going in that direction."

Chapter Nine

Managing Your Federal Career

Managing Your Federal Career

During our seven years of interviews with high-level Obama political executives, we were in a unique position to watch their mobility patterns. Of the 65 individuals we interviewed, we found that they stayed an average of three years and four months in the position to which they were confirmed. This is longer than the conventional wisdom (perhaps an urban legend) that political appointees only stay for 18 to 24 months.

We also observed an interesting phenomenon that often goes overlooked—mobility within an administration's political executive corps. We found numerous examples of individuals being promoted from within the administration. Five of the individuals we interviewed while serving as agency heads were promoted to deputy secretary (either in an acting capacity or were nominated for the position and confirmed). When one includes the tenure of individuals serving in multiple positions, the average tenure of those we interviewed was nearly four years.

Based on our observations of the comings and goings of the political executives interviewed, we gained two key insights:
- **Insight 30:** Good performance sometimes gets rewarded
- **Insight 31:** Deciding when to leave is an art

Insight 30: Good Performance Sometimes Gets Rewarded

We witnessed Obama Administration political executives take several interesting paths during the seven years we conducted interviews. While we had no access to political executives' performance assessments, we think it is safe to presume that the White House Office of Presidential Personnel took notice of a number of executives, assessed their performance as being high, and then selected them for another position within the Administration. Approximately one out of six of those we interviewed assumed another position within the Administration after we interviewed them. We think this is good practice, as it builds on the concept of experience we emphasized in Chapter Two.

We observed the following patterns of movement during the course of our project:
- **Moving up to the deputy secretary position.** Of our 65 interviewees, five were later selected to serve as deputy secretary. Three were nominated and confirmed into the position. One served as acting deputy secretary, and another is awaiting confirmation (as of March 2016). Several had very interesting journeys:
    — **Rebecca Blank** began her journey as under secretary for economic affairs, Economics and Statistics Administration in the Department of Commerce, in April 2009. She was appointed acting deputy secretary

in November 2010. She was nominated to serve as deputy secretary in November 2011 and confirmed as deputy secretary by the United States Senate in March 2012. During her time as acting deputy secretary, she also served as acting secretary of Commerce from August 2011 to October 2011. After her confirmation as deputy secretary, she once again served as acting secretary from June 2012 to June 2013. She left the Administration to become chancellor of the University of Wisconsin-Madison.
— **Patrick Gallagher,** former Director, National Institute of Standards and Technology (NIST), Department of Commerce, followed Rebecca Blank as deputy secretary. Gallagher served as acting deputy secretary and NIST director from June 2013 to July 2014. He left when Bruce Andrews was confirmed as deputy secretary and he assumed his new responsibilities as chancellor and chief executive officer of the University of Pittsburgh.
— **Victor Mendez** served as administrator of the Federal Highway Administration (FHWA), Department of Transportation, from July 2009 to December 2013. In December 2013, he was appointed acting deputy secretary and was confirmed in July 2014. In describing his transition, Mendez recalls, "Since I came from inside, it was probably not as difficult for me as it would have been for somebody outside the department. I also continued to do my FHWA job for a little while. My transition was easy because I knew all the people in the department. The agenda was pretty clear. We had seven priorities that the secretary discussed with me. My job was to help him implement those seven priorities."
— **Alejandro Mayorkas,** former Director, U.S. Citizenship and Immigration Services, Department of Homeland Security, was nominated to serve as deputy secretary of the Department of Homeland Security in June 2014, and confirmed in December 2014.
— **Mary Wakefield,** former Administrator, Health Resources and Services Administration, Department of Health and Human Services, was nominated to be deputy secretary of Health and Human Services in July 2015. As of March 2016, she was awaiting confirmation by the United States Senate.

- **Moving up one level.** A common path for political executives is to "move up" one level when the head of the agency leaves. We saw two instances of this; in both cases, there was a substantial time lag between nomination and confirmation.
  — **Michael Huerta** was confirmed as deputy administrator of the Federal Aviation Administration (FAA), Department of Transportation, in June 2010. Huerta became acting administrator in December 2011 after the resignation of his predecessor. He was nominated to become administrator in March 2012 and was confirmed in January 2013. Huerta recalls, "I was acting administrator for 13 months. This is a five-year term that got

caught up in the 2012 presidential election. There was a lot of speculation as to whether I would be nominated and whether I could get confirmed… I knew the agency pretty well by the time I was confirmed…There was a sense of relief around the agency after my confirmation. People at FAA hoped it would happen and were glad to have some certainty in continuity of leadership. After the confirmation, there was a sense that now we know how to proceed."
— **Kathryn Sullivan,** former Assistant Secretary of Commerce for Environmental Observation and Prediction, and Deputy Administrator, National Oceanic and Atmospheric Administration, Department of Commerce, served as acting NOAA administrator from February 2013 to March 2014. She was nominated to be administrator in August 2013, renominated in January 2014 (required at the start of a new Congress), and confirmed in March 2014.

- **Moving to another position after the expiration of a term appointment.** We saw two instances of this situation:
  — **Mark Rosekind,** Administrator, National Highway Traffic Safety Administration (NHTSA), Department of Transportation, served a five-year appointment as a member of the National Transportation Safety Board (NTSB). Rosekind recalls, "I was just finishing up my five-year term at NTSB and the White House was talking to me about reappointment. They also asked me whether I was interested in either of the two positions open at the Department of Transportation. I was clearly interested in the NHTSA position which they offered. As a safety guy, I understood the issues facing NHTSA."
  — **John Berry,** United States Ambassador to Australia, completed his four-year term as director of the Office of Personnel Management in April 2013. Instead of seeking renomination, the White House discussed other job opportunities for Berry in the second term. In June 2013, he was nominated to serve as ambassador to Australia and confirmed in August 2013.

- **Moving from the White House to an agency.** Another pattern we observed was the movement of White House staff (including Executive Office of the President staff) to agencies. This is a common occurrence during the second term of an administration.
  — **Christopher Lu,** Deputy Secretary of Labor, served as the White House cabinet secretary and assistant to the president from 2009 to 2013. He was nominated to be deputy secretary of labor in January 2014, and confirmed in April 2014. Lu recalls, "I had just spent four years in the White House and I knew the President's policy and management agenda pretty well. I had also been sitting on the President's Management Council in my role as cabinet secretary. So I knew a lot from my job at the White House."

— **R. Gil Kerlikowske**, Commissioner, U.S. Customs and Border Protection (CBP), served as director of the White House Office of National Drug Policy from 2009 to 2013. He recalls, "The White House asked for names of potential candidates for the CBP position. I volunteered for the job. I was eager to get back to operations and get away from policy."

Insight 31: Deciding When to Leave Is an Art

There are many different reasons for leaving a position, including personal considerations. We have found that it is important to decide how and when to leave a position. While observers might frequently remember one's first impression of an individual, they are also likely to remember their final impression of an individual based on how they handle their departure. Some appointees do it well, others do not.

Why Executives Leave
During our research and interviews, we observed the following reasons for leaving a position:
- Completion of your agenda
- Taking another position in government
- A change in the boss
- A (big) problem
- A policy disagreement
- Timing

Completion of your agenda. A reason for leaving is completing your agenda. Each political executive we interviewed had an agenda specific to their organization, and each agenda had a different timeline. In some cases, completing the agenda involves getting a piece of legislation enacted or a new law or set of regulations implemented. In other cases, it might involve a larger set of activities geared toward improving the performance of the agency and strengthening it as an institution. An individual's reputation is clearly enhanced when he or she can leave the organization with a list of specific accomplishments. Thus, there is a reputational incentive to stay long enough to complete your agenda and have accomplishments at which to point.

Taking another position in government. As discussed in Insight 30, a common reason to leave is to take another position in government. Based on our research, we conclude that this should actually happen even more than it does. By hiring from within, the administration benefits from the experience gained by political executives in their previous positions. In the five instances we saw when political executives assumed the deputy secretary position, there was obviously a much shorter learning curve than for an individual coming from outside of government in the middle of an administration.

A change in the boss. This most frequently happens when a new secretary is appointed and brings in a new team. In this case, the new secretary might want a new person in the deputy secretary slot, or the holdover deputy secretary might conclude that it is now an appropriate time to leave if he or she had been considering it. Five of the deputy secretaries we interviewed left when a new secretary was appointed in the second term of the administration. This also occurs at the deputy administrator level.

A (big) problem. As noted earlier in the book, all political executives should be ready for an unexpected event. Sometimes the unexpected event will be a large enough crisis that a change in agency leadership is required. Often, a perceived below-par performance before a congressional committee will hasten the need for change at the top of the agency.

An example of a big problem occurred in June 2015 when Office of Personnel Management (OPM) Director Kathleen Archuleta announced that there had been two major breaches in government databases holding personnel records and security-clearance files. In describing her congressional testimony, *The Washington Post* wrote, "By many accounts, Archuleta had seemed unsteady at four congressional hearings on the intrusions and failed to defend herself against criticism from lawmakers, much of it withering" (Rein and Davidson 2015). Democratic Senator Mark Warner called for Archuleta's resignation; she resigned the next day. In her letter to OPM employees announcing her resignation, Archuleta wrote, "I conveyed to the president that I believe it is best for me to step aside and allow new leadership to step in, enabling the agency to move beyond the current challenges and allowing the employees at OPM to continue their important work" (Rein and Davidson 2015). Staying in a position during a firestorm is usually not an option.

A policy disagreement. It is our impression that this happens relatively rarely. At the start of an administration there is general agreement on policies. As the administration continues, the possibility of policy disagreements arises. When it does happen, there are two scenarios: First, a policy disagreement is discussed privately and the departing appointee does not make the policy disagreement public. The second scenario is when a policy disagreement is made public and the appointee therefore resigns. To demonstrate the rarity of this reason for departing, we had to go back to 1996 to find an example from the Clinton Administration. Three high ranking political executives in the Department of Health and Human Services (Mary Jo Bane, Peter B. Edelman, and Wendell E. Primus) resigned in protest to the Personal Responsibility and Work Opportunity Act, which made significant changes in the nation's welfare system.

When Executives Leave

There are three "windows" in which political appointees most frequently leave:

Two years. Of the 65 political executives we interviewed, we found that nine served two years or less. Based on our research, key reasons individuals leave in under two years include:

- A promising job opportunity outside of government
- The job may not have "worked out" as anticipated
- An individual is asked to leave by his or her boss
- A problem arises as discussed on the previous page
- The individual must return to the institution in which they were located prior to taking their position in government (this happens most frequently to individuals previously located in academia who must return to the academic position)
- Completion of an agreed upon two year (or less) assignment

Four years. If a president is re-elected to a second term (or it is anticipated that he or she will be re-elected), the end of a first term is an ideal time to leave if one is planning a return to the private, non-profit, or academic sector. In rare instances, a re-elected White House views a second term as an opportunity to "clean house" and appoint "loyalists" throughout government (a behavior seen most clearly at the start of second term of President Richard Nixon).

Six years. For those who have completed the "long haul," the end of six years is seen as a good time to depart. Margaret Hamburg, former Commissioner, Food and Drug Administration (FDA), Department of Health and Human Services, describes her reasons to leave at the end of six years, saying, "Six years is a long time for a job like this. It's more than twice the average of an FDA commissioner in modern history. I never expected to stay this long, but I am really pleased that I was able to have a tenure that was long enough to come to understand the FDA and how it works and why it matters so much. Many things on my to-do list got checked off. Many other things are in motion, and I am confident they'll stay on track. I felt it was important for someone else to have some time to put their mark on the role of the commissioner (before President Obama's second term ends)" (Rubin 2015). Robert Califf, Hamburg's successor, was nominated in September 2015 and confirmed in late February 2016. An acting commissioner served from April 2015 to February 2016.

Summary. There is no right or wrong answer as to when to leave. It is a personal judgment based on many factors. The guidance we can provide, however, is that there is a risk to one's reputation in a short tenure (defined as less than two years). It takes at least one to two years to learn and understand an organization, as well as to begin to accumulate specific accomplishments. Without specific accomplishments, your tenure might be viewed either as "marking time" or checking off public service on your resume.

Part Two

Succeeding at the Job

Chapter Ten

Succeeding as a Deputy Secretary

Succeeding as a Deputy Secretary

We conducted interviews with 16 deputy secretaries at the departmental level. The deputy secretary job is one of the most important in government. With the passage of the GPRA Modernization Act of 2010, the position now has additional responsibilities for the management of cabinet departments.

Based on our interviews and research, we gained three insights regarding succeeding as a deputy secretary:
- **Insight 32:** The job is big—involving managing complex government organizations
- **Insight 33:** The job contains ambiguity
- **Insight 34:** Success depends on the relationship with the secretary

Insight 32: The Job Is Big—Involving Managing Complex Government Organizations

At the departmental level, the jobs of the secretary and deputy secretary are similar to running a holding company in the private sector. For example, the Department of Commerce consists of 12 agencies, 10 staff offices, and over 45,000 employees. The Department of Commerce is not alone in its size and complexity. The Department of Homeland Security has more than 240,000 employees spread among its 22 agencies. The Department of Agriculture has nearly 100,000 employees in its 29 agencies and offices.

The Department of Veterans Affairs (VA) has over 300,000 employees. In describing his job at VA, Deputy Secretary Sloan Gibson says, "I think Secretary McDonald, our chief of staff, and I have the toughest management job in America. We are a Fortune 20 company. In addition to our size, government is more complex and difficult than the private sector. This is definitely the toughest leadership job in America."

Consequently, a key role of the deputy secretary is to focus on the management of these large and complex organizations. This role has been codified in both executive orders and legislation. We found, however, that some deputies embraced the management role to a greater extent than other deputies. In most instances, the deputy secretaries with prior management experience were quicker to embrace the management role.

The concept of the deputy secretary serving as the chief operating officer (COO) of the department originated in the Clinton Administration. The official designation of COO responsibilities dates back to an October 1993 memorandum from President Bill Clinton establishing the President's Management Council (PMC) and asking each department to designate a chief operating officer. With a few exceptions (most notably the Department of the Treasury and the Department

> **The Deputy Secretary as Crisis Manager**
>
> An important role often played by the deputy secretary is as crisis manager. Former Department of the Interior Deputy Secretary David Hayes, recalls, "I was the operations lead for the department on the Gulf Oil spill. I spent every day—as did much of our team—from April 2010 to September 2010 on the oil spill." Joel Achenbach writes in *A Hole at the Bottom of the Sea* about the start of Hayes's involvement in the oil spill:
>
>> David Hayes ... arrived at his office that Wednesday morning, April 21, with no inkling that it would be anything other than a normal workday. He heard about the explosion within minutes of walking into Interior's massive building ... by mid-morning the scale of the disaster became more apparent, and Hayes's boss, Interior Secretary Ken Salazar, suggested that he jump on a plane and fly to New Orleans.
>>
>> Hayes would rather have stayed put; it was his daughter Molly's eighteenth birthday. He called his wife: "We may have a problem here."
>>
>> ... Hayes and press secretary Kendra Barkoff raced to Reagan National Airport—no luggage, not even toothbrushes—and talked their way onto a US Airways jet that had already closed its door and was about to taxi toward the runway (Achenbach 2011).

of Defense), departments designated the deputy secretary as COO. In July 2001, President George W. Bush issued a memorandum reestablishing the PMC and continuing the COO role.

In December 2010, Congress passed the GPRA Modernization Act of 2010 that codified the chief operating officer role into law. The bill, signed into law by President Obama in January 2011, states that the COO shall be responsible for improving the management and performance of the organization and "achieving the mission and goals of the agency through the use of performance planning, measurement, analysis, regular assessment of progress, and use of performance information ..." In June 2011, President Obama issued an executive order implementing the GPRA Modernization Act. The memorandum calls for the COO to be designated as the senior accountable official responsible for leading performance and management reform efforts and reducing wasteful or ineffective programs.

The 2010 law and 2011 executive order have the potential to change the role of deputy secretaries in government. One deputy secretary tells us, "I'll be interested in seeing the impact [of] the new GPRA law that says each department must name a COO. The bill also establishes a new reporting relationship to the White House. It will be interesting to see how GPRA works and how it impacts the role of deputy secretaries."

The role as department COO is one of the clearest roles that a deputy secretary can play. One deputy secretary reports, "I work on the infrastructure of the department. There are many actionable items and a bunch of moving parts. We need to work on many fronts." These fronts include working on the culture of the organization, as well as focusing on the people side of the department. All of the deputy secretaries interviewed spent time working to strengthen their Senior Executive Service corps.

In describing her role as deputy secretary of the Department of Housing and Urban Development (HUD), Nani Coloretti says, "I help the department achieve its mission by focusing on effective operations and cross-cutting policy and program issues. For example, I am working to build a stronger HUD, which means structuring the agency to address its most pressing needs in a time of declining administrative resources. The entire agency reports up to the secretary, through me" (Keegan 2015).

In describing how he views his job at the Department of Labor, Deputy Secretary Christopher Lu comments, "I often view my job as a mayor of a small town. I try to spend time talking to employees. I stop by their offices. I also go out and spend time watching what they do. I want to understand their jobs and watch them work. I believe strongly in engagement. My father was a federal employee. This engagement helps me do my job better."

In addition to working with the departmental bureaucracy, deputy secretaries spend time on interagency committees, including the President's Management Council. In describing the COO position, former Department of Veterans Affairs' Deputy Secretary Scott Gould says, "My job is really a t-shape, as I do a lot of collaboration across government with other agencies. It helps that I have a network of people I know across government. Then my job goes straight down the bureaucracy."

Finally, the continued pressure to reduce spending has increased the time deputy secretaries spend on budget-related issues. Says one deputy secretary, "The budget is going to be a problem. Resources will become increasingly scarce in the future. I think we will continue to see reductions in the budget. We have been working long hours to come up with different budget scenarios. It's always more fun when you are budgeting for a good year, but management is tough and it is our job to make tough choices. We can manage our way through this. We will end up cutting some programs."

Insight 33: The Job Contains Ambiguity

Other than the codified chief operating officer role, there is little agreement on the other components of the job. The role played by the deputy secretary is often a factor of the personal interests and background of a deputy secretary, as well as his or her relationship with the secretary. One deputy secretary tells us that after nearly two years in office, "The job of the deputy secretary is still a little unclear to me." It is our observation that the conversation between the secretary and deputy secretary about responsibilities generally did not take place. The lack of such conversations can lead to the ambiguity we identified.

One factor adding to the ambiguity of the position is the "ebb and flow" of the position between various roles over the course of a deputy secretary's tenure. Former Department of Energy Deputy Secretary Daniel Poneman remarks, "We started out on management and we spent a lot of time on that during our first year. That was very important. Then the secretary asked me to play a greater role in another area. There are also the unexpected events that nobody can predict. So you must learn to live with this ebb and flow, and you have to be ready to respond to unanticipated events."

Because of their extensive careers inside and outside government, deputy secretaries often bring a great deal of policy expertise and experience to their positions. This makes it natural for deputy secretaries to expect to play a policy role in the department. Based on our interviews and observations of deputy secretaries in previous administrations, the policy role varies dramatically from department to department.

In some cases, the deputy secretary may be asked by the secretary to participate in the policy-making process on a specific issue because of his or her expertise in that area. In other cases, a deputy secretary may be thrust into a policy-making role because of the need for a strong individual to lead the process. One deputy secretary tells us, "I had to step into the policy development and policy agenda-setting process. I ended up driving the policy process. So I had to do two-and-a-half jobs for a while. This isn't the regular job of the deputy secretary."

There are no clearly defined lines between policy and implementation; they often blend together and deputy secretaries naturally get involved in both. As one deputy tells us, "It is a combination of both a COO role and a decision-making role. Reality is that you have to do some of both. The Recovery Act forced me to get involved in both policy and implementation."

In the past, some deputy secretaries may have been attracted to Washington for the chance to work on policy issues. Because Washington has always been more of a policy town than a management town, the policy side of the deputy secretary position often has been appealing to many appointees. Over time, however, the deputy secretary position has begun to swing more toward the management role and away from the policy role.

This ambiguity of the job is only one of the factors that make the job of the deputy a difficult one. Another related factor is the challenge of keeping one's ego in check. The deputy is not to be in the limelight (the limelight is the secretary's territory). The deputy must primarily work behind the scenes and support the secretary in any task that needs to be performed. This job is obviously not for everybody (see Insight 6 for a discussion of "personality fit" to a position). One deputy secretary tells us, "I had never been a number two before, so this is a change for me. I didn't know how I would like being number two." For many deputy secretaries, this is the first time in a long time that there were not in a number one position.

Another deputy secretary describes the number-two job this way: "My major role is backing up the secretary. We want to make sure that we make the best use of his time. I'm the backstop. I'm available across the board on many issues. Your job [as deputy secretary] is to serve the secretary in whatever capacity he or she desires. I support the secretary and focus on what is important to him. That has been my view from the first day I was here."

This role includes filling in for the secretary when he or she is unavailable to attend key government meetings, and serving as "acting secretary" when necessary. As one deputy secretary tells us, "I have to be here when the secretary is out."

Insight 34: Success Depends on the Relationship with the Secretary

"There is always tension in the role between the deputy secretary and the secretary. You need to gain trust," says a former deputy secretary. While trust will be gained over time, there are clear actions that a secretary and deputy secretary can take up front to enhance the chances of a good working relationship.

The deputy secretaries we interviewed emphasize that there is no one-size-fits-all job description for a deputy secretary. All said that the job is highly dependent on the relationship between the secretary and the deputy secretary. But it does appear that administrations can do a better job in setting expectations for the position. Based on observations of previous deputy secretaries in both Democratic and Republican administrations, unmet expectations can decrease effectiveness in the job. A deputy secretary might accept the position expecting to work on policy and be surprised or disappointed to end up doing management. It is also crucial that an individual considering accepting a deputy position understands that the position is, in essence, a support position rather than a policy position.

To effectively accomplish an organization's mission, it is crucial that the secretary and the deputy secretary (and perhaps the Office of Presidential Personnel) come to a fully understood agreement on expectations for the job of the deputy secretary, and the roles that will be fulfilled by the deputy secretary. Agreement on expectations by all parties is likely to result in a more fulfilling and satisfying set of experiences for future deputy secretaries, a more effective working relationship between the secretary and deputy secretary, and accomplishing the department's agenda.

Former Secretary Kathleen Sebelius and Deputy Secretary Bill Corr formed a clear understanding of the role of the Deputy Secretary in the Department of Health and Human Services. "The Secretary is a strong leader with executive experience as governor of Kansas," Corr recalls. "From day one, she expected that she, the chief of staff, and I would operate as a team. We communicate daily, even when she is traveling, and we discuss a wide range of matters from the urgent to long-range planning…My overriding job…has been to ensure that we execute successfully."

**Recommendation:
The Secretary Should Be Given the Authority
to Select His or Her Deputy Secretary**

While this book primarily consists of insights derived from our interviews, we have concluded that the above recommendation is necessary in order to achieve an effective, productive working relationship between the secretary and the deputy secretary.

In the past, selection authority has usually solely resided in the White House. A deputy secretary position is indeed a "plum" position, but it is even more crucial that the secretary feel comfortable and have full confidence in the individual selected. (The White House would, of course, have review authority over the appointment.) In addition, the secretary should be instructed by the White House to select an individual with management experience so the deputy secretary can fulfill the crucial role of a departmental chief operating officer.

Chapter 10

Profiles-at-a-Glance
Deputy Secretaries Interviewed*

Rafael Borras
Former Under Secretary for Management, Department of Homeland Security

Confirmation Length: January 26, 2011, to April 14, 2011 (78 days)
Tenure: April 2011 to February 2014 (Two years, eleven months). Also served in a recess appointment from March 2010 to April 2011 (One year, one month). (Total tenure three years, eleven months)
Present Position: Partner, A.T. Kearney Inc.
Experience: *Federal Government* (Executive: General Services Administration; Department of Commerce); *Local Government* (Local official: New Rochelle, New York; Hartford, Connecticut; Miami-Dade County, Florida); *Non-Profit* (Executive: International City/County Management Association)

William V. (Bill) Corr
Former Deputy Secretary, Department of Health and Human Services

Confirmation Length: March 17, 2009, to May 6, 2009 (50 days)
Tenure: May 2009 to March 2015 (Five years, eleven months)
Present Position: Principal, Corr Strategies
Experience: *Federal Government* (Senate staff member; Executive: Department of Health and Human Services); *Non-Profit* (Executive: Campaign for Tobacco-Free Kids; Community-run health care centers)

---

* Indicates tenure and present position as of March 2016

W. Scott Gould
Former Deputy Secretary, Department of Veterans Affairs

Confirmation Length: March 11, 2009, to April 3, 2009 (23 days)
Tenure: April 2009 to May 2013 (Four years, one month)
Present Position: Senior Advisor, Boston Consulting Group
Experience: *Federal Government* (Executive: Department of Commerce; Export-Import Bank; Executive Office of the President), *Private Sector* (Executive: IBM; O'Gara; Exolve)

Seth D. Harris
Former Deputy Secretary, Department of Labor

Confirmation Length: March 3, 2009, to May 21, 2009 (79 days)
Tenure: May 2009 to January 2014 (Four years, nine months)
Present Position: Distinguished Scholar, Cornell University's School of Industrial & Labor Relations; Counsel, Dentons
Experience: *Academia* (Faculty: New York Law School); *Federal Government* (Executive: Department of Labor; Law clerk)

David J. Hayes
Former Deputy Secretary, Department of the Interior

Confirmation Length: February 27, 2009, to May 20, 2009 (82 days)
Tenure: May 2009 to June 2013 (Four years, one month)
Present Position: Distinguished Visiting Lecturer at Law, Stanford Law School
Experience: *Federal Government* (Executive: Department of the Interior); *Academia* (Faculty: Stanford Law School); *Private Sector* (Lawyer: Latham & Watkins)

Heather Higginbottom
Deputy Secretary of State for Management and Resources, Department of State

Confirmation Length: September 11, 2013, to December 13, 2013 (93 days)
Tenure: December 2013 to Present
Present Position: Deputy Secretary of State for Management and Resources, Department of State
Experience: *Federal Government* (Executive: Department of State; Office of Management and Budget; White House Domestic Council; Staff Member: U.S. Senate); *Non-Profit* (Executive: American Security Project; Communities in Schools)

Dennis F. Hightower
Former Deputy Secretary, Department of Commerce

Confirmation Length: July 24, 2009, to August 7, 2009 (14 days)
Tenure: August 2009 to August 2010 (One year)
Present Position: Chairman, Hightower Associates
Experience: *Private Sector* (Executive: Europe Online Networks S.A.; Walt Disney Company; Russell Reynolds Associates; Mattel; General Electric; McKinsey & Company; Xerox Research and Engineering Group); *Federal Government* (U.S. Army; Department of Defense Business Board); *Academia* (Faculty: Harvard Business School)

Maurice Jones
Former Deputy Secretary, Department of Housing and Urban Development

Confirmation Length: September 23, 2011, to March 29, 2012 (188 days)
Tenure: April 2012 to January 2014 (One year, eight months)
Present Position: Secretary of Commerce and Trade, Commonwealth of Virginia
Experience: *Private Sector* (Executive: Pilot Media; Lawyer: Hunton & Williams); *State Government* (Executive: Department of Social Services and Office of the Governor, Commonwealth of Virginia); *Federal Government* (Lawyer: Department of the Treasury; Executive: Community Development Financial Institutions Fund)

Sloan D. Gibson
Deputy Secretary, Department of Veterans Affairs

Confirmation Length: September 11, 2013, to February 11, 2014 (153 days)
Tenure: February 2014 to Present
Present Position: Deputy Secretary of Veterans Affairs
Experience: *Federal Government* (U.S. Army); *Non-Profit* (Executive: United Services Organization (USO)); *Private Sector* (Executive: AmSouth Bancorporation)

Christopher P. Lu
Deputy Secretary, Department of Labor

Confirmation Length: January 9, 2014, to April 1, 2014 (82 days)
Tenure: April 2014 to Present
Present Position: Deputy Secretary of Labor
Experience: *Federal Government* (Executive: White House; Staff Member: U.S. Senate; U.S. House of Representatives; Law Clerk); *Private Sector* (Lawyer: Sidley Austin); *Academia* (Fellow: Georgetown University School of Public Policy; University of Chicago Institute of Politics; Center for the Study of the Presidency and Congress)

Victor Mendez
Deputy Secretary and Administrator, Federal Highway Administration, Department of Transportation

Confirmation Length: May 15, 2014, to July 24, 2014 (70 days)
Tenure: July 2014 to Present
Present Position: Deputy Secretary of Transportation
Experience: *Federal Government* (Executive: Department of Transportation; Engineer: U.S. Forest Service); *State Government* (Executive: Arizona Department of Transportation)

Kathleen A. Merrigan
Former Deputy Secretary, Department of Agriculture

Confirmation Length: March 19, 2009, to April 3, 2009 (15 days)
Tenure: April 2009 to March 2013 (Three years, eleven months)
Present Position: Executive Director of Sustainability, George Washington University, and Professor of Public Policy
Experience: *Academia* (Faculty: Tufts University; Massachusetts Institute of Technology); *Federal Government* (Executive: U.S. Department of Agriculture; Staff member: U.S. Senate Committee on Agriculture, Nutrition and Forestry); *State Government* (Staff Member: Texas Department of Agriculture; Massachusetts State Senate)

Anthony (Tony) W. Miller
Former Deputy Secretary, Department of Education

Confirmation Length: May 18, 2009, to July 24, 2009 (67 days)
Tenure: July 2009 to July 2013 (Three years)
Present Position: Partner, Vistria Group
Experience: *Private Sector* (Executive: Silver Lake; LRN Corporation; McKinsey & Company; Delco Electronics); *Local Government* (Advisor: Los Angeles Unified School District; Santa Monica-Malibu Unified School District)

Thomas R. Nides
Former Deputy Secretary for Management and Resources, Department of State

Confirmation Length: September 29, 2010, to December 22, 2010 (84 days)
Tenure: January 2011 to February 2013 (Two years, one month)
Present Position: Vice Chairman, Morgan Stanley
Experience: *Private Sector* (Executive: Morgan Stanley; Burson-Marsteller; Credit Suisse First Boston); *Federal Government* (Staff member: U.S. House of Representatives; Executive: U.S. Trade Representative)

Daniel B. Poneman
Former Deputy Secretary, Department of Energy

Confirmation Length: April 20, 2009, to May 18, 2009 (28 days)
Tenure: May 2009 to October 2014 (Five years, five months)
Present Position: President and Chief Executive Officer, Centrus Energy Corp
Experience: *Private Sector* (Executive: The Scowcroft Group; Lawyer: Covington & Burling; Hogan & Hartson); *Federal Government* (Executive: Department of Energy; National Security Council)

John D. Porcari
Former Deputy Secretary, Department of Transportation

Confirmation Length: April 27, 2009, to May 21, 2009 (24 days)
Tenure: May 2009 to December 2013 (Four years, seven months)
Present Position: Senior Vice President and National Director of Strategic Consulting, WSP Parsons Brinckerhoff
Experience: *Federal Government* (Executive: U.S. Department of Transportation); *State Government* (Executive: Maryland Department of Transportation; Maryland Department of Business and Economic Development); *Academia* (Executive: University of Maryland)

Chapter Eleven

Succeeding as a Producer

Succeeding as a Producer

One of the major insights we gained during our seven years of research was the unique nature of a select group of government agencies: production agencies. While many federal government services continue to be delivered through third parties, production agencies deliver services directly to the American public. This group of agencies includes organizations such as the Social Security Administration, the Federal Aviation Administration, and the Internal Revenue Service.

Several of our interviewees used the analogy of production agencies as factories. While the factory floor is not an image commonly associated with government organizations, there is an element of manufacturing in these organizations. William Taggart, former Chief Operating Officer, Office of Federal Student Aid (FSA), Department of Education, tells us, "We needed to think like a manufacturing plant. You have to get down on the floor, wander around, see folks, and engage them."

Based on our interviews and research, we gained four insights regarding succeeding as a producer:

- **Insight 35:** Focus on outputs
- **Insight 36:** Get the metrics right
- **Insight 37:** Don't forget the customer
- **Insight 38:** Not everyone can be a producer

Insight 35: Focus on Outputs

While the image of the factory floor offered by William Taggart conjures memories of Frederick Winslow Taylor and scientific management, the comparison is very apt for production agencies. Factory managers, like the producers in government, worry about inputs, accuracy and errors, cycle time, and outputs. Factory managers aim to achieve routine and constant flow, and they pride themselves on reducing variation and increasing factory efficiency.

David Kappos, former Director, United States Patent and Trademark Office (USPTO), Department of Commerce, tells us, "We understand our inputs and outputs at USPTO." A major initiative Kappos led was to examine and reengineer the number of reviews for a patent submission. "We have good numerical data on this," says Kappos. "We want to reduce the number of reviews on a submission. We want to reduce the rewriting. We are at three reviews and we have gotten it down to between 2.3 to 2.4. The goal would be 2.0. That would be a major reduction."

We found that tracking outputs is an easily understood and powerful tool. Outputs are also a powerful tool for accountability by making public agency goals and commitments.

Insight 36: Get the Metrics Right

A key component of the producer job is getting the metrics right. When the right metrics are selected and are used to determine if the desired outputs are being delivered, they become an effective management tool for agency leadership. In the case of the Veterans Benefits Administration and the United States Patent and Trademark Office, there was an obvious metric on which the agencies were being assessed—the backlog. In the case of USPTO, the backlog was patent applications pending. Kappos set forth the goal of getting the backlog under 700,000. He felt strongly that citizens really cared about the backlog. Kappos told us, "We set the specific targets. Our goal is to get the backlog under 700,000. We haven't been under that figure for many years…We set 699,000 for FY 2011. Getting under 700,000 would be a major accomplishment." USPTO reached that goal in June 2011. In October 2015, the backlog of patents pending stood at 558,091.

For the Veterans Benefits Administration, the backlog became a major national issue. Several congressional hearings were held on the backlog, and it attracted increased media interest. To decrease the backlog, VBA mandated overtime for VBA staff. As a result, the backlog has been decreasing. In June 2013, the backlog fell below 800,000 for the first time since April 2011. The backlog total in June 2013 hit 797,801. Of those claims, 524,711 (65 percent) were backlogged more than 125 days. In September 2012, the backlog was 895,248 with over 66 percent pending for more than 125 days. The reduction in backlog was also due to a new initiative to give priority to oldest claims.

Insight 37: Don't Forget the Customer

In addition to delivering the output and getting the metrics right, another key component of the producer job is to focus on customers. Producers provide services to citizens who are eagerly awaiting a decision on a patent, a visa, a veteran's benefits, or a student loan.

This important role is highlighted by Alejandro Mayorkas, former Director of U.S. Citizenship and Immigration Services (USCIS), Department of Homeland Security. Mayorkas says, "We are essentially a customer service agency, but we did not have a way to access customer service tools. There was little experience or focus on the customer service aspect of the job." After arriving at USCIS, Mayorkas found that the agency historically had not focused on the customer service aspects of the job. This increased focus on customer service drove Mayorkas to modernize the operations of USCIS and move to greater transparency and consistency between USCIS offices. For USCIS, it is no longer a question of "production" or "quality." It is a focus on quality and all that term encompasses. Mayorkas describes this emphasis: "Speed alone cannot be the central metric when one considers our mission and everything it involves. We have to make decisions that adhere to the facts and the law, that are sound and reflect a consistent application of the law and policy, that are comprehensive in reviewing and applying the factual record, and that are thorough in detecting issues of concern."

The agency redesigned its services after a customer outreach initiative that resulted in a segmentation of customers based on their level of need:
- Those who are comfortable with the Internet and need little direct assistance from the agency
- Those who need some help
- Those who are the most vulnerable and difficult to reach

USCIS developed new programs to reach vulnerable populations, while at the same time streamlining services for customers who need less assistance.

James Runcie had a similar experience at the Office of Federal Student Aid. Runcie recalls, "I thought the agency could improve how we assess, interact, and ultimately deliver to our broadening customer base." Runcie then moved toward establishing a greater customer focus. "We wanted to increase customer awareness and make our information more accessible to them. It took us a couple of years but we made significant progress. We ultimately rebranded the organization."

As a consequence of a focus on customers, several of the political executives interviewed for our research increased efforts for segmenting their customers in order to improve service delivery. At the Department of Veterans Affairs, former Under Secretary for Benefits Allison Hickey pushed for "express lanes" for less complicated claims. Hickey recalls, "We are able to push these less complicated claims through at a faster pace. If we can do this, there will be less work on the front end ... which will then allow us to spend more time on tougher, more complicated claims. We are trying to manage our throughputs."

A major initiative at the Transportation Security Administration under former Administrator John Pistole has been the TSA Pre✓™ program, in addition to other programs that treat different segments of the traveling public differently to speed their progress through security lines. Pistole recalls, "We had been using a one-size-fits-all approach. But I knew it didn't have to be this way... I knew we were already treating people differently. I knew that there were many possibilities of doing things differently."

A final point about customer service is that customers will complain if they are not satisfied with their experience and will make their experience known. Each of the producers we interviewed found this to be true and had to devote significant time to responding to complaints, such as application backlogs or a bad experience in a TSA security line. The time spent responding to customer complaints has the potential to increase if such complaints draw the attention of the media, Congress, or stakeholder groups.

Insight 38: Not Everyone Can Be a Producer

In Chapter Two, we emphasized the importance of getting the right person into the right job. Selecting the right person for a producer position is crucial to an agency's management success. There are two components as to why everyone cannot be a producer:
- **Experience:** Prior management experience is indeed crucial for assuming leadership and providing direct services to the public.
- **Working style:** We found that there is indeed a unique working style that serves producers well in delivery-type organizations.

Experience. Nearly all of the producers we interviewed brought relevant backgrounds and expertise to their government positions. Most importantly, they served in leadership positions directing activities similar to those they would direct in government. As noted earlier, Kappos spent his career in intellectual property at IBM. David Stevens, former Commissioner, Federal Housing Administration (FHA), Department of Housing and Urban Development, came from a real estate and banking background, including working at Freddie Mac. William Taggart came to FSA from the banking industry. Their prior private-sector careers had prepared them well for their government positions. In reflecting on his selection, Stevens says, "I understood the business. I had lots of experience in the business. Some of the previous incumbents had not really understood the industry. I was one of the few commissioners in this position who had practical industry experience."

Historically, many previous appointees selected to run production-type agencies came to their positions with strong policy backgrounds. Their experience in the private sector was often limited or nonexistent. While there were business leaders who were selected as cabinet secretaries over the years, the sub-cabinet has been largely dominated by "policy types." The shift from the hiring of policy types to "managerial types" began to pick up momentum in Washington during the 1990s, with a growing recognition that managerial experience is often exactly the type of experience needed to run many government organizations.

Working style. In addition to their managerial or business experience, there is also a working style that serves producers well in these types of agencies. This working style can be characterized as:
- Hard-charging and high-energy
- Disciplined and focused on delivering the outputs of the organization
- Data-oriented
- Engagement-oriented, reflected in their outreach to employees as seen in the holding of town hall meetings, visiting regional offices, and regularly communicating with employees via blogs or newsletters.

Just as there is a desired professional background and working style for the ideal producer, there are also working styles that might *not* be conducive to leading production organizations. Such working styles might include:
- A tendency to like working on and focusing primarily on "big issues"

- Low to moderate interest in the nitty-gritty details of the organization's operations
- Low to moderate interest in reaching out to meet with or communicate with the organization's frontline workers
- Preference to work primarily in their offices with personal and headquarters staff

Profiles-at-a-Glance
Producers Interviewed*

Randy Babbitt
Former Administrator, Federal Aviation Administration, Department of Transportation

Confirmation Length: May 11, 2009, to May 21, 2009 (10 days)
Tenure: June 2009 to December 2011 (Two years, seven months)
Present Position: Senior Vice President of Labor Relations, Southwest Airlines
Experience: *Private Sector* (Executive: Oliver Wyman; Eclat Consulting; ALPA; Pilot: Eastern Airlines)

Allison A. Hickey
Former Under Secretary for Benefits, Veterans Benefits Administration, Department of Veterans Affairs

Confirmation Length: January 5, 2011, to May 26, 2011 (141 days)
Tenure: June 2011 to October 2015 (Four years, four months)
Present Position: Chief Executive Officer, All In Solutions LLC
Experience: *Private Sector* (Executive: Accenture); *Federal Government* (U.S. Air Force)

---

* Indicates tenure and present position as of March 2016

Michael Huerta
Administrator, Federal Aviation Administration, Department of Transportation

Confirmation Length: March 27, 2012, to January 1, 2013 (280 days)
Tenure: January 2013 to Present
Present Position: Administrator, Federal Aviation Administration
Experience: *Private Sector* (Executive: 2002 Olympic Winter Games; Affiliated Computer Services); *Local Government* (Executive: New York City Department of Ports, International Trade and Commerce; Port of San Francisco); *Federal Government* (Executive: Department of Transportation)

David J. Kappos
Former Under Secretary of Commerce for Intellectual Property, and Director, U.S. Patent and Trademark Office, Department of Commerce

Confirmation Length: June 18, 2009, to August 7, 2009 (50 days)
Tenure: August 2009 to February 2013 (Four years, six months)
Present Position: Partner, Cravath, Swaine & Moore
Experience: *Private Sector* (Executive: IBM)

TJ Kennedy
Former Acting General Manager, FirstNet, Department of Commerce

Confirmation Length: Member of the Senior Executive Service (Confirmation not required)
Tenure: July 2013 to Present
Present Position: President, FirstNet
Experience: *Private Sector* (Executive: Raytheon; SAIC; Intermountain Healthcare); *Local Government* (Park City Fire District); *State Government* (Utah Department of Public Safety)

R. Gil Kerlikowske
Commissioner, U.S. Customs and Border Protection, Department of Homeland Security

Confirmation Length: January 6, 2014, to March 6, 2014 (90 days)
Tenure: March 2014 to Present
Present Position: Commissioner, U.S. Customs and Border Protection
Experience: *Local Government* (Police Executive: Seattle, Washington; Buffalo, New York; St. Petersburg, Florida); *Federal Government* (Executive: Office of National Drug Control Policy; Department of Justice)

Alejandro N. Mayorkas
Former Director, U.S. Citizenship and Immigration Services, Department of Homeland Security

Confirmation Length: May 20, 2009, to August 7, 2009 (79 days)
Tenure: August 2009 to December 2013 (Four years, four months)
Present Position: Deputy Secretary, Department of Homeland Security (as of March 2016)
Experience: *Private Sector* (Lawyer: O'Melveny & Myers LLP); *Federal Government* (Lawyer: U.S. Attorney's Office for Central District of California)

John T. Morton
Former Director, U.S. Immigration and Customs Enforcement, Department of Homeland Security

Confirmation Length: March 10, 2009, to May 12, 2009 (63 days)
Tenure: May 2009 to June 2013 (Four years, one month)
Present Position: Senior Vice President, Capital One
Experience: *Federal Government* (Lawyer: Department of Justice; U.S. Attorney's Office; Immigration and Naturalization Service)

Robert A. Petzel
Former Under Secretary for Health, Veterans Health Administration, Department of Veterans Affairs

Confirmation Length: November 18, 2009, to February 11, 2010 (85 days)
Tenure: February 2010 to May 2014 (Four years, three months)
Experience: *Federal Government* (Department of Veterans Affairs); *Academia* (Faculty: University of Minnesota Medical School)

John S. Pistole
Former Administrator, Transportation Security Administration, Department of Homeland Security

Confirmation Length: May 17, 2010, to June 25, 2010 (39 days)
Tenure: June 2010 to December 2014 (Four years, six months)
Present Position: President, Anderson University (Indiana)
Experience: *Federal Government* (Executive: Federal Bureau of Investigation)

Leon Rodriguez
Director, U.S. Citizenship and Immigration Services, Department of Homeland Security

Confirmation Length: January 7, 2014, to June 24, 2014 (168 days)
Tenure: July 2014 to Present
Present Position: Director, U.S. Citizenship and Immigration Services
Experience: *Federal Government* (Executive: Office of Civil Rights, Department of Health and Human Services; Department of Justice; U.S. Attorney's Office); *Local Government* (Lawyer: Montgomery County, Maryland; Kings County District, New York); *Private Sector* (Lawyer: Ober, Kaler, Grimes & Shriver)

James W. Runcie
Chief Operating Officer, Office of Federal Student Aid, Department of Education

Confirmation Length: Member of the Senior Executive Service (Confirmation not required)
Tenure: September 2011 to Present
Present Position: Chief Operating Officer, Office of Federal Student Aid
Experience: *Federal Government* (Department of Education); *Private Sector* (Executive: UBS Investment Bank; Banc of America Securities Corporation; Donaldson, Lufkin & Jenrette Securities Corporation; Xerox Corporation)

David H. Stevens
Former Assistant Secretary for Housing, and Commissioner, Federal Housing Administration, Department of Housing and Urban Development

Confirmation Length: April 20, 2009, to July 10, 2009 (81 days)
Tenure: July 2009 to March 2011 (One year, eight months)
Present Position: President and Chief Executive Officer, Mortgage Bankers Association
Experience: *Private Sector* (Executive: Long & Foster Companies; Freddie Mac; Wells Fargo; World Savings Bank)

William J. Taggart
Former Chief Operating Officer, Office of Federal Student Aid, Department of Education

Confirmation Length: Presidential appointment without Senate confirmation (PA appointment, confirmation not required)
Tenure: June 2009 to July 2011 (Two years, one month)
Experience: *Private Sector* (Executive: Veritas One Consulting, LLC; Wachovia Corporation; First Union Corporation; IBM)

Michael Whitaker
Deputy Administrator, Federal Aviation Administration, Department of Transportation

Confirmation Length: Member of the Senior Executive Service (Confirmation not required)
Tenure: May 2013 to Present
Present Position: Deputy Administrator, Federal Aviation Administration
Experience: *Private Sector* (Lawyer: TWA; Executive: United Airlines; InterGlobe Enterprises)

Chapter Twelve

Succeeding as a Regulator

Succeeding as a Regulator

Serving as a government regulator involves unique management challenges and direct engagement with groups with different interests. Based on our interviews, we gained the following insights regarding succeeding as a regulator:
- **Insight 39:** Be prepared for contention
- **Insight 40:** Get the rules out
- **Insight 41:** Respond to unexpected events
- **Insight 42:** Don't forget your stakeholders

Insight 39: Be Prepared for Contention

The job of the regulator is highly contentious. New regulators should be prepared for this contention and have prior experience in managing strongly held, diverse views. Public and congressional attitudes toward regulation are highly volatile and subject to wide swings in support depending on the current political environment. Inez Tenenbaum, former Chair of the Consumer Product Safety Commission (CPSC), tells us, "It has been a roller coaster. We have so many contentious issues. Many of our rulemaking initiatives were mandated by Congress … I was expecting a more positive environment. I wasn't expecting so much conflict."

Coupled with a politically contentious environment is the high visibility that comes with being a regulator. Tenenbaum says, "I've been surprised at the high visibility and high profile of the agency. Many of our issues—cribs, baby bumpers, window coverings—have received much attention." Even one year after the Deepwater Horizon explosion, Michael Bromwich, former Director, Bureau of Ocean Energy Management, Regulation and Enforcement (BOEMRE), Department of the Interior, was surprised "at the great press attention and political intensity that surrounded our issuing of permits. Things are somewhat quieter right now in summer 2011, but not much."

One of the compelling findings from our research is that regulatory agencies differ in degrees of contention between board members in those agencies. At the Federal Energy Regulatory Commission, former Chairman Jon Wellinghoff describes a non-contentious five-member commission that, he says, "does not think in partisan terms. We look at rates and make judgments." At the Nuclear Regulatory Commission, former Chairman Allison Macfarlane observes that differences of opinion between commissioners are not partisan, but more a matter of professional judgment. Macfarlane says, "Our 'ideology'—if we can call it that—is over nuclear issues. Commissioners bring different regulatory and technical perspectives to their work. Our internal procedures drive us to work through these differences."

Insight 40: Get the Rules Out

Due to the nature of the job, regulators have both policy and management responsibilities. In a five-member commission, the chairman becomes the individual responsible for managing the organization in addition to his or her responsibilities as a voting member of the commission. At the CPSC, Tenenbaum's responsibilities included running the organization, managing the rulemaking process, and voting on the rules that the commission will issue. Former Administrator David Strickland, National Highway Traffic Safety Administration (NHTSA), Department of Transportation, was charged with getting the rules out and serving as the leader of the organization.

Both Tenenbaum and Strickland took on the major initial activity of speeding up their agencies' process for getting new rules out. Tenenbaum describes one of her initial actions at the agency: "I told our staff and the Office of General Counsel to pick up the pace. Everything was simply taking too long. The delays were burdensome on industry. Industry needed to know what we were going to do so they could be ready to respond." Strickland expresses a similar frustration: "It was taking six months to elicit comments on some of our rules. We didn't have that long. We had to speed it up." The job of managing the rulemaking process falls to the agency administrator or the chair. In the chair model, individual commission members have little or no responsibility for oversight of the speed and management of the rulemaking process.

Insight 41: Respond to Unexpected Events

The purpose of regulations is to minimize the potential for disasters, such as the Deepwater Horizon and Upper Branch explosions; therefore it should not come as a surprise when unexpected events occur in a regulated industry. The challenge then becomes effectively responding to the crisis. If your agency does not already undertake "gaming" exercises to plan for an unexpected event, you should consider undertaking such "games" early in your tenure.

Two of the political executives we interviewed—Joseph Main at the Mine Safety and Health Administration (MSHA), Department of Labor, and Bromwich at BOEMRE—faced a major national crisis during their tenures. Main confronted the challenge of investigating and responding to the Upper Big Branch mine explosion that occurred in April 2010, six months after his confirmation in October 2009. Bromwich arrived at BOEMRE in June 2010, two months after the Deepwater Horizon explosion and subsequent environmental crisis, with a charge to serve both as a crisis manager and a turnaround manager for the organization.

Strickland and Tenenbaum also faced crises, albeit somewhat less dramatic ones. Strickland arrived at NHTSA in January 2010, in the middle of the Toyota recall crisis. When Tenenbaum arrived at CPSC in 2009, the organization was still responding to the aftermath of the 2007 recall of Chinese-made toys contaminated with lead paint.

If (or when) a crisis hits, regulators must continue to run their organizations while dealing with the crisis. In effect, their workload doubles and they act in the roles of both crisis manager and chief executive officer concurrently. Main recounts, "I'm very proud that I was able to keep the agency running in spite of Upper Big Branch. We had a successful strategy in place and we kept it going. We kept doing our work..."

In reflecting on his experience at BOEMRE, Bromwich recalls that he not only had to deal with the immediate aftermath of the Deepwater Horizon crisis, but also faced the challenge of reorganizing the agency, getting the permits issuance process running again, and getting the organization's employees back on track.

Insight 42: Don't Forget Your Stakeholders

Each regulatory agency has its own distinct set of stakeholders, all of whom make their views well known. It is possible to map each regulatory organization's stakeholders, which range from citizens/consumers to corporations to foreign governments. While most regulatory agencies interact with regulated industries, there is a group of regulatory agencies that deals directly with citizens. These agencies include NHTSA and the CPSC. In the case of NHTSA, Strickland recounts meeting with families of individuals who have died in car crashes. "They come to meet with me," says Strickland. "It gives me a sense of the importance of my job."

Tenenbaum spent much time with corporations. "I have been reaching out to stakeholders, instead of waiting for them to come to me," Tenenbaum recounts. "I want to work with companies on voluntary standards. Voluntary standards are the first step. We let industries regulate themselves, unless their regulations are ineffective. Sometimes voluntary standards are too little and too late. We want the stakeholders to come talk to me and the other commissioners. I have really reached out to industry. I must talk to an industry representative three or four times a day."

Tenenbaum's efforts in reaching out to industry paid off. An article in *The New York Times* describing her tenure at CPSC emphasized that before Tenenbaum could make headway on child safety issues, she "had to persuade consumer advocates that she would work for them while reassuring manufacturers that the agency would not be unfair in carrying out its new powers. It was a difficult juggling act that some industry officials say Ms. Tenenbaum has managed to pull off. 'What I was most glad about is that she treated industry as a resource, rather than the enemy,' said Carter Keithly, president of the Toy Industry Association. 'We didn't agree on everything, but she was always fair'" (Nixon 2013).

Many of these discussions also require great sensitivity. Former Commissioner Margaret Hamburg describes her experience at the Food and Drug Administration: "We expect companies to give us information. Companies do not want that information discussed publicly. We need to be aware of what is for public consumption and what is not. However, we still want more transparency. We want to increase trust in the agency. We are getting stakeholders involved and sharing information."

Profiles-at-a-Glance
Regulators Interviewed*

Elizabeth Birnbaum
Former Director, Minerals Management Service, Department of the Interior

Confirmation Length: Member of the Senior Executive Service (Confirmation not required)
Tenure: July 2009 to May 2010 (Ten months)
Present Position: Principal, SEB Strategies LLC
Experience: *Non-Profit* (Lawyer: National Wildlife Federation; American Rivers); *Federal Government* (Lawyer: Department of the Interior; Staff Member: U.S. House Committee on Natural Resources; U.S. House Committee on House Administration)

Michael R. Bromwich
Former Director, Bureau of Ocean Energy Management, Regulation and Enforcement, Department of the Interior

Confirmation Length: Member of the Senior Executive Service (Confirmation not required)
Tenure: June 2010 to November 2011 (One year, five months)
Present Position: Managing Principal, The Bromwich Group
Experience: *Private Sector* (Lawyer: Fried, Frank, Harris, Shriver & Jacobson; Mayer, Brown & Platt; Foley & Lardner); *Federal Government* (Executive: Department of Justice; Lawyer: Independent Counsel for Iran-Contra; U.S. Attorney's Office)

* Indicates tenure and present position as of March 2016

J. Dudley Butler
Former Administrator, Grain Inspection, Packers and Stockyards Administration, Department of Agriculture

Confirmation Length: Member of the Senior Executive Service (Confirmation not required)
Tenure: May 2009 to January 2012 (Two years, eight months)
Present Position: Attorney at Law, Butler Farm and Ranch Law Group
Experience: *State Government* (Lawyer: Office of Governor Cliff Finch; Mississippi Department of Corrections); *Private Sector* (Lawyer: Farm and Ranch Law Group)

Margaret Hamburg
Former Commissioner, Food and Drug Administration, Department of Health and Human Services

Confirmation Length: March 25, 2009, to May 18, 2009 (54 days)
Tenure: May 2009 to April 2015 (Five years, eleven months)
Present Position: Foreign Secretary, Institute of Medicine, National Academy of Sciences
Experience: *Non-Profit* (Executive: Nuclear Threat Initiative); *Local Government* (Executive: New York City Department of Health and Hygiene); *Federal Government* (Executive: Department of Health and Human Services; National Institutes of Health)

Abigail Ross Hopper
Director, Bureau of Ocean Energy Management, Department of the Interior

Confirmation Length: Member of the Senior Executive Service (Confirmation not required)
Tenure: January 2015 to Present
Present Position: Director, Bureau of Ocean Energy Management
Experience: *State Government* (Executive: Maryland Energy Administration; Maryland Public Service Commission); *Private Sector* (Lawyer: Hogan Lovells; Joseph, Greenwald and Laake)

Allison M. Macfarlane
Former Chairman, Nuclear Regulatory Commission

Confirmation Length: May 24, 2012, to June 29, 2012 (36 days)
Tenure: July 2012 to December 2014 (Two years, six months)
Present Position: Professor of Public Policy and International Affairs, and Director, Center for International Science and Technology Policy, The George Washington University
Experience: *Academia* (Faculty: George Mason University; Georgia Tech)

Joseph A. Main
Assistant Secretary of Labor for Mine Safety and Health, Director of Mine Safety and Health Administration, Department of Labor

Confirmation Length: July 6, 2009, to October 21, 2009 (107 days)
Tenure: October 2009 to Present
Present Position: Assistant Secretary of Labor for Mine Safety and Health, and Director of the Mine Safety and Health Administration
Experience: *Private Sector* (Independent Consultant; Executive: United Mine Workers of America)

Mark Rosekind
Administrator, National Highway Traffic Safety Administration, Department of Transportation

Confirmation Length: November 19, 2014, to December 16, 2014 (27 days)
Tenure: December 2014 to Present
Present Position: Administrator, National Highway Traffic Safety Administration
Experience: *Federal Government* (Executive: National Transportation Safety Board; Scientist: National Air and Space Administration); *Private Sector* (Executive: Alertness Solutions); *Academia* (Research Faculty: Stanford University)

David Strickland
Former Administrator, National Highway Traffic Safety Administration, Department of Transportation

Confirmation Length: December 4, 2009, to December 24, 2009 (20 days)
Tenure: December 2009 to December 2013 (4 Years)
Present Position: Partner, Venable LLP
Experience: *Federal Government* (Staff Member: U.S. Senate Committee on Commerce, Science, and Transportation)

Inez Moore Tenenbaum
Former Chairman, Consumer Product Safety Commission

Confirmation Length: June 9, 2009, to June 19, 2009 (10 days)
Tenure: June 2009 to November 2013 (Four years, five months)
Present Position: Attorney at Law, Inez Moore Tenenbaum, LLC
Experience: *Private Sector* (Lawyer: McNair Law Firm; Sinkler & Boyd, P.A.); *State Government* (Executive: South Carolina State Superintendent of Education; Elected official: South Carolina House of Representatives); *Non-Profit* (Lawyer: South Carolina Center for Family Policy)

Jon B. Wellinghoff
Former Chairman, Federal Energy Regulatory Commission

Confirmation Length: December 11, 2007, to December 19, 2007 (8 days)
Tenure: January 2009 to November 2013 (Four years, eleven months)
Present Position: Partner, Stoel Rives LLP
Experience: *Private Sector* (Lawyer: Beckley Singleton; Efficient Energy Systems, Inc.); *Federal Government* (Staff member: U.S. Senate Committee on Commerce, Science and Transportation; Lawyer: Federal Trade Commission); *State Government* (Executive: Consumer Advocate for Customers of Public Utilities; Lawyer: Nevada Public Utilities Commission); *Local Government* (Lawyer: Office of the District Attorney for the County of Washoe, Nevada

Chapter Thirteen

Succeeding as a Science Executive

Succeeding as a Science Executive

While nearly every federal department funds research and development projects, there is a group of federal agencies primarily dedicated to research, statistics, and analysis in specific scientific disciplines. We call these organizations the science agencies, led by individuals whom we have termed science political executives.

Based on our interviews with science executives, we gained the following insights:
- **Insight 43:** Maintain the scientific integrity of the organization
- **Insight 44:** Interface with the political leadership of the organization
- **Insight 45:** Make the organization relevant to government decision-making
- **Insight 46:** Reach out to external stakeholders

Insight 43: Maintain the Scientific Integrity of the Organization

All the science executives we interviewed for our project emphasize the importance of scientific integrity. They all tell us that there is no margin of error in this role. Marcia McNutt, former Director, U.S. Geological Survey (USGS), Department of the Interior, says, "You need a strong firewall between USGS and the political chain of command. There is tension between keeping our peer-reviewed scientific studies independent until they are ready to be released. We share these scientific studies with the political appointees in the department. I need to keep them informed and give them a heads-up at the appropriate time." Richard Newell, former Administrator, U.S. Energy Information Administration (EIA), Department of Energy, comments, "I have to be sensitive not to blindside any of our political people on EIA reports." While needed by all political executives, good judgment and a sensitive political antenna are crucial for science political executives to maintain their credibility in both the scientific and political communities.

After discussing their concern about potential conflicts between the scientific integrity of their organization and politics, none of the science political executives interviewed report any instances of political interference during their tenure. "I've been surprised," says McNutt, "at how rarely politics have intervened. We were involved in the Recovery Act. I didn't receive any requests for specific projects. We were doing what was right."

While government's science civil servants clearly recognize that politics is a component of life in government, there is great sensitivity to "too much politics." Patrick Gallagher, former Director, National Institute of Standards and Technology (NIST), Department of Commerce, recalls, "In administrations of recent years, the position of NIST director seemed somewhat more political than in the past—which it had never been before. That was a little unsettling to folks here, so they are glad now to be back in the days when a career person was selected for the presidential appointment as director."

Insight 44: Interface with the Political Leadership of the Organization

Science political executives must know the administration and their secretary's agenda, in addition to determining how their organization can help move that agenda along. In many cases, this requires the science political executive to make key connections with other political executives and to "work the process." McNutt says that she spent more than 60 percent of her time working closely with the Office of the Secretary and other political appointees in the Department of the Interior.

Science political executives must also to know when there is a problem within the organization. The executive must then determine whether that problem needs to be brought to the attention of the department's political team. Rebecca Blank, former Under Secretary for Economic Affairs, Economics and Statistics Administration (ESA), Department of Commerce, describes her experience with the 2010 Census: "We have a good team on this. Nancy Potok, Deputy Under Secretary at ESA, has done the day-to-day oversight, so I've spent less time on this than I had imagined. I am brought in when there is a problem to deal with."

Insight 45: Make the Organization Relevant to Government Decision-Making

All the science political executives interviewed made great efforts to increase the relevance of their organization. In her position near the top of the Department of Commerce, Blank spent much of her time talking with key individuals in the White House, the Council of Economic Advisors, and the National Economic Council to better understand their economic information needs. As a result of Blank's interactions with policy makers, the White House asked her organization to produce several key studies for them.

Science political executives walk a fine line between wanting to be relevant and helpful and not distorting their historic mission. This tension was clearly seen in Gallagher's participation in the administration's review of cybersecurity and the development of new policies in this area. "I was concerned that the issue of cybersecurity might change the role of NIST," says Gallagher. "We have a clear role to play on the technology side of the issue. We did not, however, want to be put in the position of setting policy rules. That isn't the role of NIST. We need to continue to do what we do best. I worry about mission creep.

I understand what my organization can add and I know our capabilities. Key is understanding your role."

Newell sought to encourage greater use of EIA data by the department while avoiding any hint of politicizing the data. "I want EIA to be viewed as independent," says Newell, "and we want to be a place where the department can seek advice. I want EIA to do more analysis and help the department more. We don't advocate, we analyze. I want us to provide input into policy making and provide higher quality analysis … It is important to note that our vision statement says that we are independent. We want to be impartial, but not irrelevant."

Insight 46: Reach Out to External Stakeholders

Kathryn Sullivan described the importance of external stakeholders in her role as acting administrator of the National Oceanic and Atmospheric Administration (NOAA). Sullivan told *The Washington Post,* "Now that I'm in the lead seat, I understand more clearly the dynamics and importance of stakeholder engagement and the degree to which, in an agency like NOAA, there are many entities that feel they fully share the agency's passion and purpose and have an expectation of being accorded some kind of participation in the decision-making. The day I took the helm as acting administrator, I had our folks pull together a list of our most valued stakeholders, and I penned a short, handwritten note to each introducing myself, commenting how honored I was to be tapped as acting, and assuring them that I knew of our partnership and their concerns.

"I got back e-mails and personal notes appreciating the fact that a NOAA administrator, acting or not, would reach out—not driven by an issue or a need—just to say 'I'm here. I know you're there. It matters to me that we're connected and that you know I care about that connection'" (Fox 2013).

Science political executives serve as the main liaison to their relevant scientific organization. Blank recalls, "There are a number of groups who care about the Bureau of Economic Analysis and the Census Bureau, such as the American Statistical Association. I speak to those groups." Shortly after her confirmation as director of the United States Geological Survey, McNutt spoke to the American Geological Association.

Profiles-at-a-Glance
Science Executives Interviewed*

Peter H. Appel
Former Administrator, Research and Innovative Technology Administration, Department of Transportation

Confirmation Length: April 20, 2009, to April 29, 2009 (9 days)
Tenure: April 2009 to September 2011 (Two years, five months)
Present Position: Director, Alix Partners
Experience: *Private Sector* (Executive: A.T. Kearney, Amtrak); *Federal Government* (Executive: Federal Aviation Administrator)

Rebecca M. Blank
Former Under Secretary for Economic Affairs, Economics and Statistics Administration, Department of Commerce

Confirmation Length: April 28, 2009, to May 21, 2009 (23 days)
Tenure: June 2009 to June 2013 (Four years)
Present Position: Chancellor, University of Wisconsin-Madison
Experience: *Academia* (Faculty: University of Michigan; University of Michigan's National Poverty Center; Northwestern University/University of Chicago Joint Center for Poverty Research; Princeton University; Massachusetts Institute of Technology); *Federal Government* (Economist: Council of Economic Advisors)

---

* Indicates tenure and present position as of March 2016

Patrick D. Gallagher
Former Director, National Institute of Standards and Technology, and Under Secretary of Commerce for Standards and Technology, Department of Commerce

Confirmation Length: October 7, 2009, to November 5, 2009 (29 days)
Tenure: November 2009 to August 2014 (Four years, nine months)
Present Position: Chancellor and Chief Executive Officer, University of Pittsburgh
Experience: *Federal Government* (Executive: National Institute of Standards and Technology)

Erica L. Groshen
Commissioner, Bureau of Labor Statistics, Department of Labor

Confirmation Length: February 17, 2012, to January 2, 2013 (320 days)
Tenure: January 2013 to Present
Present Position: Commissioner, Bureau of Labor Statistics, Department of Labor
Experience: *Federal Government* (Economist: Federal Reserve Bank of New York; Federal Reserve Bank of Cleveland); *Academia* (Faculty: Columbia University); *International* (Economist: Bank for International Settlements); *Private Sector* (Economist: Abt Associates; Mathematica Policy Research)

Marcia K. McNutt
Former Director, U.S. Geological Survey, Department of the Interior

Confirmation Length: August 4, 2009, to October 21, 2009 (78 days)
Tenure: October 2009 to February 2013 (Three years, four months)
Present Position: Editor-in-Chief, *Science*
Experience: *Non-Profit* (Executive: Monterey Bay Aquarium Research Institute); *Academia* (Faculty: Massachusetts Institute of Technology; Stanford University; University of California, Santa Cruz); *Federal Government* (Scientist: United States Geological Survey)

Richard G. Newell
Former Administrator, U.S. Energy Information Administration, Department of Energy

Confirmation Length: May 18, 2009, to July 31, 2009 (74 days)
Tenure: August 2009 to July 2011 (One year, eleven months)
Present Position: Professor and Director, Energy Initiative, Duke University
Experience: *Academia* (Faculty: Duke University; Harvard University); *Federal Government* (Economist: Council of Economic Advisors); *Non-Profit* (Economist: Resources for the Future); *Private Sector* (Economist: ICF Incorporated)

Kathryn D. Sullivan
Assistant Secretary of Commerce for Environmental Observation and Prediction, and Deputy Administrator, National Oceanic and Atmospheric Administration, Department of Commerce

Confirmation Length: January 5, 2011, to April 14, 2011 (99 days)
Tenure: April 2011 to March 2014
Present Position: Under Secretary of Commerce for Oceans and Atmosphere, and Administrator, National Oceanic and Atmospheric Administration
Experience: *Academia* (Executive: Ohio State University); *Non-Profit* (Executive: Center of Science and Industry); *Federal Government* (Scientist: National Oceanic and Atmospheric Administration; National Aeronautics and Space Administration)

John Thompson
Director, United States Census Bureau, Department of Commerce

Confirmation Length: May 23, 2013, to August 1, 2013 (70 days)
Tenure: August 2013 to Present
Present Position: Director, United States Census Bureau, Department of Commerce
Experience: *Private Sector* (Executive: National Opinion Research Center, University of Chicago); *Federal Government* (Executive: Bureau of the Census)

Chapter Fourteen

Succeeding as an Infrastructor

Chapter 14

Succeeding as an Infrastructor

During our interviews for this project, we discovered an interesting set of agencies that have responsibility for developing and enhancing the nation's economic infrastructure. These agencies are seeking new ways to provide energy, highways, broadband, and railroads. In different ways, each is focused on developing a crucial aspect of the nation's infrastructure. Because of their information-sharing role and educational role, we labeled this group as the infrastructors. We gained the following insights from our interviews from this group of political executives:
- **Insight 47:** Outreach is key
- **Insight 48:** Get the money out

Insight 47: Outreach is Key

All the political executives interviewed in this group of agencies had substantial outreach responsibilities. They all had to collaborate with their stakeholder groups, as well as educate them on the government's funding availability for infrastructure. All viewed information sharing with stakeholders as a key part of their jobs.

A major responsibility for these agencies is outreach to state governments, industry, applicants for funding, and the recipients of their funding. Building the nation's infrastructure is not a "hands-off" activity. At the Rural Utilities Service (RUS) in the Department of Agriculture, staff was active in reaching out to organizations that had not applied in the first round of applications. Former RUS Administrator Jonathan Adelstein recalls, "We got people to apply in the second round who had not applied in the first round. We developed an interactive process in which we communicated more effectively with potential grantees. This process led to the outcomes we desired. We got some good applications. We wanted to encourage the right people to apply." In addition to reaching out to new applicants, RUS sent selected first-round submissions (which had not been accepted) back to applicants to be revised and resubmitted in the second round. These efforts, believes Adelstein, resulted in improved applications in the second round.

State government is a significant stakeholder for many agencies. Because of his background as director of the Arizona Department of Transportation, former Federal Highway Administration (FHWA) Administrator Victor Mendez brought the perspective of a state transportation official to the Department of Transportation headquarters in Washington. A major priority for Mendez was to find new ways for FHWA to engage with the states. One new vehicle for FHWA was the Every Day Counts (EDC) program. As part of that program, FHWA partnered with the Association of State Highway Transportation Officials to host 10 regional innovation summits. The summits are a vehicle for FHWA to disseminate EDC strategies and technologies.

The Federal Railroad Administration (FRA) had to take an aggressive role in reaching out to states to assist them in completing the stakeholder agreements with rail owners or rail operators, who would operate the proposed projects—a key requirement to receiving Recovery Act funding. Former FRA Administrator Joseph Szabo recalls, "We thought the states and the private sector would be able to negotiate the agreements, but that wasn't happening. We had to help them on their service agreements. We helped get them to where they needed to be." This involvement followed an aggressive outreach at the start of the program. FRA held listening sessions with key stakeholders at which they explained the high-speed rail initiative and received feedback on the program.

Outreach was also high on the agenda of Arun Majumdar, former Director, Advanced Research Products Agency-Energy (ARPA-E), Department of Energy, during his first year. A major part of his job was reaching out to the community in two-way conversations—both to learn what the community was doing and to inform the community of federal government funding opportunities. Majumdar recalls, "I reached out to universities. I set up informal meetings to just chat with experts to find out their issues and thoughts. I wanted to know what people were already doing."

The outreach role is also seen in working with Congress. Majumdar says, "I tell them (Congress) what we do. I like to explain our agency in laymen's terms. I try to make it easy for them to understand and talk to them in terms of impacts and savings, which gives them the big picture."

Insight 48: Get the Money Out

All political executives in this group of agencies have to aggressively manage their organizations to produce the expected results. During the time period in which our interviews were taking place, these agencies were working hard to get federal funds out quickly in response to the Recovery Act. At FRA, Szabo had to borrow staff from other parts of the Department of Transportation to handle the increased workload. Szabo, like Adelstein, had to work with his agency to speed it up and make it more flexible. They had to closely manage their organizations' inputs and outputs and make sure all the tasks associated with the Recovery Act were completed in a timely, efficient, and transparent manner.

Chapter 14

Profiles-at-a-Glance
Infrastructors Interviewed*

Jonathan S. Adelstein
Former Administrator, Rural Utilities Service, Department of Agriculture

Confirmation Length: April 21, 2009, to July 24, 2009 (94 days)
Tenure: July 2009 to September 2012 (Three years, three months)
Present Position: President and Chief Executive Officer, PCIA-The Wireless Infrastructure Association
Experience: *Federal Government* (Executive: Federal Communications Commission; Staff member: U.S. Senate; U.S. Senate Committee on Aging)

Arun Majumdar
Former Director, Advanced Research Projects Agency-Energy, Department of Energy

Confirmation Length: September 21, 2009, to October 21, 2009 (30 days)
Tenure: October 2009 to June 2012 (Two years, eight months)
Present Position: Jay Precourt Professor, Stanford University, faculty member of the Department of Mechanical Engineering, and co-director of the Precourt Institute for Energy
Experience: *Academia* (Executive: Lawrence Berkeley National Laboratory; Faculty: University of California, Berkeley; University of California, Santa Barbara; Arizona State University)

* Indicates tenure and present position as of March 2016

Victor M. Mendez
Deputy Secretary, and Former Administrator, Federal Highway Administration, Department of Transportation

Confirmation Length: April 23, 2009, to July 10, 2009 (78 days)
Tenure: July 2009 to July 2014 (Five years)
Present Position: Deputy Secretary of Transportation
Experience: *State Government* (Executive: Arizona Department of Transportation); *Federal Government* (Engineer: U.S. Forest Service)

Peter M. Rogoff
Former Administrator, Federal Transit Administration, Department of Transportation

Confirmation Length: April 29, 2009, to May 21, 2009 (22 days)
Tenure: May 2009 to January 2014 (Three years, seven months)
Present Position: Chief Executive Officer, Sound Transit, Seattle, Washington
Experience: *Federal Government* (Staff Member: U.S. Senate Committee on Appropriations)

Joseph C. Szabo
Former Administrator, Federal Railroad Administration, Department of Transportation

Confirmation Length: March 26, 2009, to April 29, 2009 (34 days)
Tenure: April 2009 to January 2015 (Five years, eight months)
Present Position: Senior Fellow, Chicago Metropolitan Agency for Planning
Experience: *Private Sector* (Executive: United Transportation Union; American Federation of Labor and Congress Industrial Organizations); *State Government* (Elected Official: Riverdale, Illinois)

Chapter Fifteen

Succeeding as a Collaborator

Succeeding as a Collaborator

While we believe that all political executives need collaborative skills, there are some political executives whose jobs require a high degree of collaboration. In our interviews, we discovered a group of political executives whom we call the collaborators. Based on our interviews, we gained the following insights from these executives:
- **Insight 49:** Collaborate with other organizations
- **Insight 50:** Leverage the use of federal funds

Insight 49: Collaborate with Other Organizations

We found two situations in government where political executives must effectively collaborate:
- **The central management agency collaborator with responsibility for working across government.** Prime examples of this type of collaboration are those working in central management agencies, such as the Office of Management and Budget (OMB), the Office of Personnel Management (OPM), and the General Services Administration.
- **The small agency collaborator with limited funding and staff.** Because their funding and staffing levels are limited, these political executives need to create collaborations with other federal agencies, state and local government, the private sector, and the non-profit community.

The central management agency collaborator. While former Director John Berry might have been able to give orders (when he chose to do so) within the Office of Personnel Management, his influence across the government was based on his collaboration skills. In describing the unique challenge of getting interagency clearance on many of his initiatives and policies, Berry says, "This is a responsibility that most other agencies do not have to undergo. We have to get approval from OMB and then also get approval by agencies. We need 26 agencies to say 'yes.' Any of them can say 'no.'" Berry worked hard to get input from his colleagues across government in the development of new policies and initiatives. By the time a document is ready for the clearance process, Berry has often touched base with all the key actors in departments across government. The interagency collaborative work is crucial to the success of OPM in its role as policy leader. Berry elaborates, "I work closely with the Chief Human Capital Officer's Council and the President's Management Council, as well as the cabinet."

David Mader, Controller, Office of Management and Budget, Executive Office of the President, emphasizes his partnership role with other departments and agencies. Mader says, "I work very closely with the Department of Treasury and the General Services Administration. I am executing our strategic plan with our partner agencies. The key to this job is learning how to manage through others."

We created teams to work with clients. It is much like my experience in consulting. Shared services is a good example of working with departments and agencies. Our job is to convince government folks of a different way to do business. Like all organizations, some people are more supportive than others."

G. Edward DeSeve, Senior Advisor to the President for Recovery Act Implementation, demonstrated during his tenure the collaborator skills in introducing a network approach to overseeing the Recovery Act. DeSeve recalls, "I sat down with Vice President Biden. He wanted me to be the CEO of the activity. I said I didn't think it was a CEO job. Instead, I thought it was more of a coordinator job. My job was to work with the White House and the agencies. I had no direct authority and a small staff. It's not like when I was deputy director for management at OMB, which I had a statute behind me...We are working a new form of government organization, networked government...We could not be authoritarian or command and control in this position. Being General Patton would not work in this position." DeSeve put in place networks between agencies, between agencies and recipients, between agencies and the White Houses, and between grantees and overseers.

The small agency collaborator with limited funding and staff. At the Department of Health and Human Services' Substance Abuse and Mental Health Services Administration, Pamela Hyde faced the challenge of collaborating with other agencies. Hyde states, "Lots of other agencies do part of what we do. Regarding substance abuse and mental illness, there is hardly anything we do that somebody else is not also doing." Thus, the challenge facing all small agency collaborators is developing effective working relationships with other federal agencies. These agency heads need to maximize their potential impact by enlisting other federal agencies in the accomplishment of their goals.

David Hinson at the Department of Commerce's Minority Business Development Agency (MBDA) and Raymond Jefferson at the Department of Labor's Veterans' Employment and Training Service (VETS) spent a significant part of their time working with other government agencies after taking on their positions. Both MBDA and VETS were created to serve as "spurs" and leaders in government for their respective missions. Hinson and Jefferson had to carve out roles and activities in which their agencies could contribute in a crowded field of agencies, all of which have some "piece of the action" in their policy areas.

For Jefferson, the veterans' field was indeed crowded. Other government agencies involved with veterans include the Office of Personnel Management (involved in the hiring of veterans within government), the Department of Veterans Affairs (involved in providing benefits to veterans via the Veterans Benefits Administration), and the Department of Defense (with its myriad offices related to veterans). There has long been a discussion as to whether VETS should be moved to the Department of Veterans Affairs or remain in the Department of Labor. In navigating between these various other government agencies, Jefferson recalls, "Sometimes I feel that I am conducting shuttle diplomacy."

Insight 50: Leverage the Use of Federal Funds

The leveraging of federal dollars is a key tool in the playbook for the Health Resources Services Administration (HRSA) in the Department of Health and Human Services. A major component of former Administrator Mary Wakefield's job was to effectively leverage federal dollars to accomplish national health objectives. A prime example of leveraging federal dollars is HRSA's $4 million grant to the University of Minnesota to create a Coordinating Center for Interprofessional Education and Collaborative Practice. The Coordinating Center will support research, education, data collection, and analysis on the use of well-functioning, well-coordinated teams to provide better patient and family outcomes. In addition to the $4 million federal grant, HRSA enlisted the support of four private philanthropies that committed an additional $8.6 million to support Center projects. Thus, a $4 million grant grew to a $12.6 million project.

A similar approach is used in the Fish and Wildlife Service (FWS). The mission of FWS is "working with others to conserve, protect, and enhance fish, wildlife, plants, and their habitats for the continuing benefit of the American people." This mission is accomplished through a wide variety of partnerships. FWS notes that throughout its history, the agency has been committed to a collaborative approach to conservation. The agency has created partnerships with local municipalities, private landowners, school groups, corporations, state governments, federal agencies, and numerous other groups and organizations. Like other collaborative agencies that need to create partnerships with organizations outside of the federal government, FWS uses a variety of mechanisms to achieve its partnership activities, including grants and cooperative agreements, memoranda of understanding, donations, and statutory partnerships.

In describing his activities, Daniel Ashe, Director of the U.S. Fish and Wildlife Service, Department of the Interior, says, "We are now working to strengthen our relationships with professional communities. We reached out to our legacy partners. We wanted to know what they wanted and what they expected. We found that they wanted to be part of our team. They wanted a more consistent relationship. They are significant communities. We now have a more diverse set of communities with whom we interact. We need to develop more mechanisms for participation."

Profiles-at-a-Glance
Collaborators Interviewed*

Daniel M. Ashe
Director, U.S. Fish and Wildlife Service, Department of the Interior

Confirmation Length: January 5, 2011, to June 30, 2011 (176 days)
Tenure: June 2011 to Present
Present Position: Director, U.S. Fish and Wildlife Service
Experience: *Federal Government* (Executive: U.S. Fish and Wildlife Service; Staff member: U.S. House Committee on Merchant Marine and Fisheries)

John Berry
Former Director, Office of Personnel Management

Confirmation Length: March 4, 2009, to April 3, 2009 (30 days)
Tenure: April 2009 to April 2013 (Four years)
Present Position: United States Ambassador to Australia
Experience: *Federal Government* (Executive: National Zoological Park; Department of the Interior; Department of the Treasury; Smithsonian Institution; Staff member: United States House of Representatives); *Non-Profit* (Executive: National Fish and Wildlife Foundation); *State Government* (Staff member: Maryland State Senate Finance Committee)

* Indicates tenure and present position as of March 2016

Doug Criscitello
Former Chief Financial Officer, Department of Housing and Urban Development

Confirmation Length: November 11, 2009, to February 11, 2010 (92 days)
Tenure: February 2010 to August 2011 (One year, six months)
Present Position: Executive Director, Center for Finance and Policy, Massachusetts Institute of Technology
Experience: *Local Government* (Executive: New York City Independent Budget Office); *Federal Government* (Executive: Office of Management and Budget; Congressional Budget Office); *Private Sector* (Executive: J.P. Morgan Securities Inc.; Grant Thorton LLP; PricewaterhouseCoopers LLP)

G. Edward DeSeve
Former Special Advisor to the President for Recovery Act Implementation

Confirmation Length: Presidential appointment without Senate confirmation (PA appointment)
Tenure: February 2009 to January 2011 (One year, eleven months)
Present Position: Executive in Residence, Brookings Institution Executive Education Program
Experience: *Federal Government* (Executive: Department of Housing and Urban Development; Office of Management and Budget); *State Government* (Executive: Commonwealth of Pennsylvania); *Local Government* (Executive: City of Philadelphia); *Private Sector* (Executive: Public Financial Management; KPMG; Merrill Lynch Capital Markets); *Academia* (Faculty: University of Maryland; University of Pennsylvania)

David A. Hinson
Former National Director, Minority Business Development Agency, Department of Commerce

Confirmation Length: Member of the Senior Executive Service (Confirmation not required)
Tenure: July 2009 to January 2014 (Four years, six months)
Present Position: Chief Financial Officer and Chief of Mergers & Acquisitions, MicroTechnologies, LLC
Experience: *Private Sector* (Executive: Wealth Management Network, Inc.; Envestnet Asset Management; Bank of America; Morgan Stanley & Company; J.P. Morgan Chase)

Brad Huther (Deceased)
Former Chief Financial Officer, Department of Housing and Urban Development

Confirmation Length: March 13, 2014, to September 17, 2014 (188 days)
Tenure: September 2014 to June 2015 (9 months)
Experience: *Federal Government* (Executive: U.S. Department of Commerce); *Academia* (Faculty: American University); *Private Sector* (International Intellectual Property Institute; World Intellectual Property Organization)

Pamela Hyde
Former Administrator, Substance Abuse and Mental Health Services Administration, Department of Health and Human Services

Confirmation Length: October 5, 2009 to November 20, 2009 (46 days)
Tenure: December 2009 to August 2015 (Five years, eight months)
Experience: *State Government* (Executive: New Mexico Human Services Department; New Mexico Job and Family Services Department; Ohio Department of Mental Health); *Local Government* (Department of Housing and Human Services, Seattle, Washington); *Non-Profit* (Executive: Community Partnership for Behavioral Health Care)

Raymond M. Jefferson
Former Assistant Secretary for Veterans' Employment and Training Service, Department of Labor

Confirmation Length: June 3, 2009, to August 7, 2009 (65 days)
Tenure: August 2009 to July 2011 (One year, eleven months)
Experience: *Private Sector* (Executive: McKinsey & Company); *State Government* (Executive: Hawaii Department of Business, Economic Development, and Tourism); *Federal Government* (Department of Commerce; U.S. Army)

David Mader
Controller, Office of Management and Budget, Executive Office of the President

Confirmation Length: May 5, 2014, to July 17, 2014 (73 days)
Tenure: July 2014 to Present
Present Position: Controller, Office of Management and Budget (former Acting Deputy Director for Management, June 2015 to November 2015)
Experience: *Private Sector* (Executive: Booz Allen Hamilton; Sirota); *Federal Government* (Executive: Internal Revenue Service)

Rhea Suh
Former Assistant Secretary for Policy, Management, and Budget, Department of the Interior

Confirmation Length: April 20, 2009, to May 18, 2009 (28 days)
Tenure: May 2009 to September 2014 (Five years, four months)
Present Position: President, Natural Resources Defense Council
Experience: *Federal Government* (Executive: Department of the Interior; Staff member: United States Senate); *Non-Profit* (Executive: David and Lucile Packard Foundation; The William and Flora Hewlett Foundation)

Mary K. Wakefield
Former Administrator, Health Resources and Services Administration, Department of Health and Human Services

Confirmation Length: Member of the Senior Executive Service (Confirmation not required)

Tenure: February 2009 to March 2015 (Six years, one month)

Present Position: Acting Deputy Secretary, Department of Health and Human Services

Experience: *Academia* (Faculty: University of North Dakota; Executive: Center for Health Policy, Research and Ethics, George Mason University); *Federal Government* (Staff member: United States Senate)

Part Three

Perspectives from Europe

Chapter Sixteen

Insights from European Executives

Succeeding as a Political Executive: Perspectives from Europe

By Arnauld Bertrand, EY Global Government & Public Sector (GPS) Advisory Leader

Through seven high-level interviews, we highlighted the lifecycle of a public sector executives mandate in France and Germany to identify the pitfalls executives face and advantages they can leverage: from appointment and preparation to the critical first 100 days and professional development prospects.

Whilst public executives certainly face unique challenges due to the complexity of public policies and organizations, they also possess specific advantages as they mostly move in the same public area. However, these advantages do not appear to be fully leveraged.

New positions can "fall into the lap" of high-level civil servants because of the natural high turnover rate of managerial posts in the public sector (as often as every two to three years). Without a prolonged confirmation period or a system of deferred appointments, appointees in Europe have little time to acquaint themselves to their new positions.

Succeeding in the Transition

The most common approach executives adopt is to reach out to predecessors who are accessible to their successors (which is not always the case for their private sector counterparts). However, this practice is far from the norm; some benefit from substantial contacts with their predecessors, whereas many have little or no contact. With no formalised transition mechanisms in place, it comes down to the context of the transition and the personalities involved. When they do happen, hand-off meetings prove to be valuable starting points, even if the parties do not share a common vision or political affiliation.

In complex administrations with large political and social issues, we believe that these informal conversations should be replaced by organized preparation including formal state of play, organized handover, deffered appointments, and meetings among peers to better prepare new executives during their transition.

Such organized transitions should strengthen a new executive's ability to define a vision and a strategy for the administration. This seems important, as many executives lack a clear roadmap due to speedy appointments or to lack of political vision definition.

The Need for a 100-Day Roadmap

In the upper echelons of the civil service, as on the political level, it is imperative to enter a new position with a clear roadmap. With circumstances most often excluding the time for extensive preparation, executives have limited time to develop this. Moreover, they fret that there is often a lack of a concrete political vision to serve as a framework (or a lack of communication between political and administrative levels). This arises in part from an undeveloped dialogue between the political and administrative levels, with politically-sensitive ministerial cabinets often playing middle-man between ministers and their directors.

Often lacking clear political vision, effective public executives may have difficulty seeing through the tumult of their daily work demands, reflecting on what they want their organisation to look like in the future, and translating this into clear objectives.

Even more than in private companies, the first 100 days of a new public executive's mandate are critical to sustainably putting into motion real change. Moreover, there is an urgent sense that the transition period provides an often all-too-rare opportunity to evolve and thus must be exploited. However, this transition period is as treacherous as it can be fruitful.

We found that an important balancing act is required to find the elusive equilibrium between effecting positive change and doing too much, too fast. With little time for preparation, the first 100 days are also a crash course in a new organisation or field of activity. This means that even meticulously prepared "plans of attack" can be sidelined by the constant effort needed to understand the job.

Moreover, most public executives are faced with the prospect, at least once in their career, of taking up a position in a field completely foreign to them. The natural reflexes and instincts a manager honed over his or her career still prove valuable, but they must often play catch-up during the initial (crucial) period of their mandate. In these circumstances, public executives are particularly prone to having their credibility undermined. It is important for executives to maintain an inquisitive mindset and demonstrate that they are open to *and* interested in understanding what makes an organisation tick.

A common regret that often surfaces in such starting times is becoming bogged down in operational details and losing touch with the meta-objectives fixed at the outset. Executives must concentrate on priorities and focus on "peaks over 3,000 feet."

Despite the close proximity to their peers, leading positions can often be solitary ones with few opportunities to compare notes with peers and learn from each other's experiences. Public management could take advantage of the size of the public sector to develop formal fora for these sorts of exchanges and more effectively structure leadership growth trajectories.

Recommendations

Based on our interviews, we developed four areas of improvement for top executive management during a transition:

Recommendation One: Public performance would take advantage of deferred appointments and systematised cooperation between incoming and outgoing executives to create more space for them to familiarise themselves with their new position.

Recommendation Two: Better managed transitions will create more favourable conditions for executives to be able to identify their priorities and construct a concrete roadmap prior to assuming their responsibilities, particularly for the critical first 100 days.

Recommendation Three: A clear political mandate and close fluid relationships between the administrative and political levels is an important enabling factor for public executives. This can be facilitated, for example, through the establishment of ExComs bringing together political and administrative counterparts.

Recommendation Four: Executive positions in the public sectors have a unique and common set of challenges, but remain too often closed off from their peers. Creating opportunities for executives to interact and exchange with their peers is important for honing leadership and managerial skills and exchanging best practices.

Arnauld Bertrand is an Advisory Partner of Ernst & Young et Associés based in Paris (France). He also serves as EY Global Government & Public Sector (GPS) Advisory Leader and World Bank Account International Leader.

Previously, Arnauld Bertrand has led GPS activities for the French, Luxemburg, and Maghreb EY regions and was the EY Global Public Finance Management (PFM) Leader.

Arnauld has 21 years of experience working for the public sector with public finance management, cost reduction, public policy and organization evaluation, public performance improvement, and transformation programs mainly for federal administrations and international donors.

Insights from European Executives

Interview with Pascal Faure
Chief Executive of the General Directorate for Business (French Tax Administration)

Interviewer: Arnauld Bertrand

About Pascal Faure

Since December 2012, Pascal Faure has served as Director General for Enterprise (DGE).

He began his career in research and development at BELL Laboratories (United States), before working with Apple, and then the National Center for Telecommunications Studies as project leader in communications security and cryptology.

From 1992 to 1995, he worked at the French Ministry of Budget, overseeing state expenditure in the field of public administration IT. He was then named technical councilor in the cabinet of the Minister for Tourism before joining the cabinet of the Minister for Territorial Development, Cities and Integration.

From 1997 to 2001, Pascal Faure occupied the post of director of development, financial affairs and deputy to the administrator-general of the Telecommunications Institute. He was then named deputy technical director at the Ministry of Defense. In parallel, he served as President of the Association of Telecommunications Engineers from 2001 to 2006. From 2007 to 2012, Pascal Faure was vice president of the General Council for the Economy, Industry, Energy and Technology.

A graduate of Paris's *Ecole nationale supérieure des télécommunications de Paris*, Pascal Faure also attended the *Ecole polytechnique*.

Q. Once you were appointed, how did you start preparing for your new role?

A. I didn't have much time to prepare because the decision to appoint me as chief of the General Directorate was made only shortly before I effectively took on my duties. However, I had the advantage of knowing the administration and the people.

Based on my experience, I would encourage appointments with a deferred effective start date (in periods other than political transition periods such as presidential elections, legislative elections, etc. so as to not to hamper a new majority's latitude for action).

Q. Can you describe your first three months in this function?

A. The political roadmap was pretty clear (the chief executive is directly chosen by the Minister) with leeway for the chief executive to bring the administration in line with the objectives set, e.g. setting up a sub-directorate dedicated to handling businesses in recovery.

The appointed chief executive effectively has 100 days in which to set the tone and give new sense of purpose to actions to be taken. I believe the periods for making changes in the public sector do not arise often, which makes it necessary to strike the right balance between acting quickly and getting the big picture, and between overdoing it and deadlock. It is especially difficult at the beginning of the presidential term of office as a result of usually difficult-to-handle toxic files, related to electoral pledges made, files that often go against the mainstream and are politically divisive. At the same time, there is a new team coming on board that may be wary of the administration.

Q. What advice do you have for political executives?

A. I think chiefs executive should more often be selected based on two criteria: expertise and leadership. The latter should be taken into consideration and there should also be a proven experience in a ministry cabinet, for optimum handling of the managerial specifics, priorities, and the time spent on political issues. It is essential for the chief executive to keep the overall picture in mind except on certain highly sensitive files. The juggling of collective, individual, strategic, and specific issues is key. In addition, to be efficient, it is crucial to have direct contact with the Minister.

There is now an interesting initiative for the Prime Minister's Office underway to renew the state governing framework. This framework includes:
- Systematic appointments with all the chiefs executive appointed to the Ministerial Council
- Proposed in-depth coaching program
- Peer group seminars (three per year)

I also believe that it is very useful to set up an executive committee with the minister, the chief of staff, deputy chief of staff, secretary general, and the chiefs executive in order to have a strong ExCom in close connection with the minister.

About the Direction Générale des Entreprises (DGE) (www.entreprises.gouv.fr)

Under the authority of the Minister for the Economy, Industry and Digital Affairs, the DGE is tasked with developing and implementing government policy for industry, the digital economy, tourism, commerce, craft industries, and trades and services.

The DGE's 1,300 staff members work nationally and regionally to promote business start-ups, growth, innovation, and competitiveness for companies of all sizes in France and abroad. The DGE also works in close partnership with businesses and business representatives, including trade organisations and federations, chambers of commerce, industry and trade, and support networks.

Interview with Jérôme Filippini
General Secretary of the Court of Auditors

Interviewers: Arnauld Bertrand and Delphine Roy

About Jérôme Filippini

A former student of the *Ecole normale supérieure, Sciences Po* Paris and the *Ecole nationale d'administration*, Jérôme Filippini began his career in 1996 as an auditor in the French Court of Accounts, which is the French Supreme Audit Institution. Promoted in 1999, he worked closely with the first president and became then the deputy secretary general of the Court from 1999 to 2001.

Filippini was then appointed to the Ministry of Interior, where he served as a deputy prefect, general secretary of the Tarn-et-Garonne Prefecture from 2001 to 2003. He then joined the logistics department of the police prefecture in Paris, where he set up and led the Administration and Modernization Division until 2006. He was deputy director for the organization and oversaw the functioning of the "deconcentrated" services of the Prison Administration at the Ministry of Justice (2006–2007). Then as advocate general of the Court of Accounts (2007–2009), he was charged with the management of the Ministry of Interior's IT and communication systems between 2009 and 2011.

He then occupied a number of functions in the field of inter-ministerial coordination and State reform. In 2011 and 2012, he served as deputy to the secretary general of the government and inter-ministerial director of IT and communication systems. He pioneered the position of chief information officer (CIO) for the French government, a position he held until November 2012. In parallel, he led the French government's talent management program. In October 2012, he was appointed secretary general for government modernization. In November 2013, he was appointed by presidential decree as the new secretary general of the Court of Auditors.

Q. Once you were appointed, how did you prepare to take up your duties?

A. For the SGMAP (*Secrétariat Général pour la Modernisation de l'Action Publique*—General Secretariat for the Government Modernization), my appointment was the result of positive maturation with several years of work on state reform and the proposed merger of the DGME (*Direction Générale de la Modernisation de l'Etat*—General Directorate for State Modernization), the DISIC (*Direction Interministérielle des Systèmes d'Information et de Communication*—State Chief Information Officer), and Etalab (state agency for open data policy). I was also able to exchange briefly with my predecessor before his departure.

At the government seminar announcing the establishment of the SGMAP, I expected a clear roadmap and a strategic policy vision, but there was certainly at that time a lack of coherent policy vision or an operational roadmap.

Taking up my duties at the Court of Auditors (*Cour des comptes*) was calmer. I was very familiar with the institution, I had more time for training, to meet the teams, and exchange with the first president of the Court.
- The very short delay before taking up office is a problem. There is not enough time to plan ahead before the official appointment. Appointments should have a deferred effective date, like at Defense or for diplomatic posts, where duties are taken up six months later. The opposite example is préfet (prefect) positions.

Q. Tell us about your first three months in this position.

A. Experience as secretary general helps you to have the tools needed to take up these duties, but the major issue was relations with politicians, although that is a major factor for a head of an administration (and I had never worked in a ministerial cabinet before).

At the Court of Auditors I was able to have a number of exchanges with my predecessor. I did a three-month progress report and proposed a three-year action plan. However, at the SGMAP I saw very little of my predecessor (we spent one afternoon together), I wrote no activity report for the first three months and I did not have time to take a step back and reflect—everything was done in a rush. I worked with the prime minister's teams, but not with the prime minister himself.

However, upon my arrival at the SGMAP, I did have a "minister file" put together by my predecessor, which gave a very accurate report on the situation.
- Ministers should work directly with their key members of staff and their directors. There should be a relationship of trust between a politician and his administration.
- It is important to be able to exchange among peers, for example in seminars. Best practices are more developed now, but not enough. Central Administration Director (CAD) seminars between peers—24 hours with 25 participants—are organized by the prime minister's departments.
- It is important to have a mission statement (check the mandate if it is not clear) and a clear roadmap with a strategic vision.

Q. How did you organize your time during the first year?

A. Organizing your time is difficult but is a priority. You have to take account of both the short- and long-term strategic vision.

It is essential to carve out time for reflection and organization. This makes the selection of close collaborators of primary importance. These collaborators ensure oversight and make it possible for you to organize your working time, which is not easy in the initial months when everything is moving very quickly. Thus, no three-month discovery report, due to lack of time.
- The ability to choose one's collaborators is key for a manager. If needed, reorganization of the inner team should be facilitated.
- There is a need to make recruitment methods objective by calling on hiring professionals, defining the background needed, drawing up a job description,

and setting up selection committees (goal: clarifying how selections are made). Other recommendations:
- Reform ministerial cabinets with cabinets made up of GS/GDs, four or five policy advisors, the director and head of cabinet.
- Move toward a spoils system ensured by the central administration directors.

About the Court of Auditors

The Court of Auditors is an independent body responsible for auditing the use of public funds in France. It is independent from the government and the parliament. It has financial jurisdiction and is in charge of auditing, issuing rulings, and certifying the state and social security account, as well as contributing to the evaluation of public policies. The Court publishes and makes available on its website all of its work.

Interview with Dr. Jürgen Gehb
Spokesman of the Board of the German Institute for Federal Real Estate

Interviewers: Dr. Fritjof Börner and Birgit Neubert, both EY Germany

About Dr. Jürgen Gehb

Dr. Jürgen Gehb has been Spokesman of the Board of the German Institute for Federal Real Estate since August 2010. Prior to his present position, he was a member of the German Bundestag from 1998 to 2009. He has also served as Mayor of Kassel, Germany, a judge at the Administrative Court in Kassel, and a judge at the Hess Administrative Court.

Dr. Gehb studied law at the Phillips-Universität in Marburg, Germany, and subsequently did practical legal training. He graduated from Georg-August-Universität, Göttingen with a doctorate in law.

Q. How did you prepare for your new role?

A. There wasn't a lot of time for preparation! The previous head of the Institute for Federal Real Estate retired. And I took over even before I had been given a letter of appointment or an employment contract. Really, the job just fell into my lap. When I first started I would sometimes come into the office and simply not know what to expect.

Q. What areas did you focus on during the first three months?

A. I was pretty much thrown into the deep end, so I started by trying to find out about my new role in general. And on the theoretical side, I succeeded fairly quickly. I took a look at the history of the Institute for Federal Real Estate in parliament and talked to insiders. It was established on January 1, 2005, as a direct federal institution under public law subject to the supervision of the Federal Ministry of Finance. The Institute for Federal Real Estate succeeded the Federal Property Administration, which existed for over 50 years, with its various federal property offices, forestry offices, and property departments of the regional finance offices. This administration was dismantled and its responsibilities and staff were transferred. Unlike the Federal Property Administration, the Institute for Federal Real Estate operates as a value-based and commercially managed business—a paradigm shift which I found myself in charge of implementing. This required a fundamental change in thinking and it still does.

I also tried to make myself known within the organization. We have offices scattered all over Germany—from Freiburg in the south to Rostock in the north, and from Aachen in the west to Frankfurt an der Oder in the east. The structure is a bit like a spider web. The head office is located in Bonn. Then there are nine directorates and around 120 smaller units. I wanted to find out what kind of people worked for the Institute for Federal Real Estate and how the organization ticks. That was the part of my new role I enjoyed most because here my duty and my inclination coincided. I enjoy the exchange with our employees as well as with our customers.

I have also been lucky to have two colleagues on the board with whom I have had a very good working relationship right from the start.

Q. What were the biggest challenges you faced?

A. I felt that the purpose and significance of our work did not bear any relation to the recognition that the Institute for Federal Real Estate was receiving. We have a portfolio of 25,000 properties, some 490,000 hectares of land, and 38,000 housing units, which makes us one of the largest owners of real estate in Germany. The Institute for Federal Real Estate has faced numerous new challenges since it was founded. Currently, we are investing substantial efforts in support for the provision of emergency housing to refugees and asylum seekers. The structural reform of the German Armed Forces and the conversion of land vacated by foreign forces previously stationed in Germany is another important job facing the Institute for Federal Real Estate. Working in close cooperation with local authorities, numerous large areas of land have to be converted from military to civil use.

We are also responsible for the administration and centralized management of real estate on behalf of the federal government entities as well as the acquisition of nearly all federal government real estate in Germany. The properties are then rented out to the entities in return for the standard local rent. Some of the federal government entities were not very happy about this at first.

Another challenge was to improve the image of the Institute for Federal Real Estate.

Q. You mean the public perception was less favorable than the reality?

A. Yes, exactly. I think the packaging should tell you something about what's inside. My responsibilities also include media and public relations. For example, not long after I took office, I started organizing regular parliamentary evenings. My motto is: "Don't just do good, talk about it!"

Q. Did you have any goals for your first year in office? Or for the years after that?

A. Yes, I did and I still do. Over the last 10 years, the Institute for Federal Real Estate has become the government's central real estate provider. We now own, with a few exceptions, all real estate used by the German federal government. Nearly all government entities have now signed rental agreements.

Another job is to meet the demand for land and buildings for federal government purposes, either by building ourselves or in the context of public-private partnerships, or by buying or renting properties. The goal I have set for myself here is to continue to fast-track these processes in the future.

Also, the Institute for Federal Real Estate is about to undergo an internal organizational restructuring.

Q. Do you think you used your first year in the job as well as you could have?

A. As well as I could have, yes, as well as was possible, no. However, I don't know whether I could have done anything very differently. Overall, I think the beginning went extremely well. Over the last few years we have developed into an efficient and modern service provider for government real estate. Our focus is on professional marketing of the government's assets. This includes making the appropriate investments to enhance the value of our properties.

Q. Will demographic change lead to a lack of qualified workers for the Institute for Federal Real Estate in the future?

A. I'm not particularly worried about that. We have some 6,500 employees at different locations in Germany. The work is varied and demanding. Many young people who join us today have a bachelor's degree in real estate management. We may not be able to compete with the salaries offered in the private sector, but we can offer our staff jobs that are secure and offer opportunities for growth.

Q. Were you sometimes frustrated in your first year when things didn't change as quickly as you would have liked them to?

A. Everyone who knows me knows that patience is not exactly one of my strengths (laughs). But I'm not one to get frustrated either, I've got too much of a cheerful disposition for that. I always go to work with a spring in my step. But you do need to have staying power.

Thank you for your time, Dr. Gehb.

> **About the Institute for Federal Real Estate**
> **(www.bundesimmobilien.de)**
>
> The Institute for Federal Real Estate is the central real estate service provider to the German federal government. The Institute manages approximately 25,000 properties, 490,000 hectares of land, and 38,000 housing units. The Institute has real estate assets valued at 22.4 billion euros.
>
> The Institute manages the overwhelming majority of the property used by the federal government for its work. It employs roughly 6,500 people in its business divisions, divided between its registered office in Bonn and more than 120 main offices and local branches throughout Germany.

Interview with Tanja Gönner
Chair of the Management Board of the Deutsche Gesellschaft für Internationale Zusammenarbeit GmbH (GIZ)

Interviewers: Dr. Fritjof Börner and Birgit Neubert, both EY Germany

> **About Tanja Gönner**
>
> Tanja Gönner has been Chair of the Management Board of Deutsche Gesellschaft für Internationale Zusammenarbeit GmbH (GIZ) since July 2012. Prior to her present position, she was a member of the state parliament of Baden-Württemberg. During her career, she has served in the following positions of the state of Baden-Württemberg: minister for the environment, nature protection and transport; environmental minister; and minister of social affairs. She has also served as a member of the German Bundestag.
>
>
>
> Gönner studied law at the Eberhard-Karls University, Tübingen. In 1997, she completed her First State Examination in Law, followed by serving as an articled clerk at the Ravensburg district court. In 1999, she completed the Second State Examination in Law and was admitted to the German bar.

Q. How did you prepare for your new role? Did you contact your predecessor?

A. Before I was appointed to the GIZ Management Board, I had an initial meeting with my predecessor and then two more following my appointment by the Supervisory Board, which was most helpful. Furthermore, in the first three months in my new role, I frequently discussed things with my predecessor, who explicitly made himself available to this end during that time.

In addition, my predecessor's farewell, which I was invited to, took place one week before I started and gave me the opportunity to get to know some of the employees in person.

Q. How were your first 100 days in office?

A. Successfully heading an organization is a question of trust for me. On the one hand, it is about trust in your own capabilities and the ability to focus on the right areas. But it is also a matter of trust in the capabilities and skills of the staff, and of the core management team in particular. For this reason, I immediately began to speak with the various managers across the board in Germany and in other countries about where we stand, where we want to go, and what challenges lie ahead.

Q. What did you choose to focus on, having obtained this initial overview?

A. We are a service provider for the German government, and most of our contracts come from German ministries. As a former politician, speaking with our partners in Berlin was the easy part, as I knew most of the people concerned and am still in touch with them.

What was new for me was our business activities in other countries. I approached this in two stages: First of all, and without it being widely known, I went on a one-week exposure visit where I was given the chance to take part in a project in Morocco. Secondly, I made a conscious decision to visit one or two key countries in each continent where we operate. My first official business trip took me to two countries where we have a very large portfolio and where security is a big challenge, namely Pakistan and Afghanistan. I then traveled to Africa, to Uganda and South Sudan, followed by a trip to India, one of the largest emerging economies in Asia. And then finally to Latin America, to Honduras and El Salvador.

Q. Were there any goals that you hoped to achieve by the end of your first year in your new role or in a wider context?

A. GIZ came into being following a merger only one-and-a-half years before I joined the company. For that reason, the obvious challenge was to form one GIZ out of its three predecessor organizations. In retrospect, we made far more progress far more quickly than we thought we would back then. In a second step, it was important to place the company on a solid long-term footing. To this end, my colleagues on the board and I deliberately took the necessary time before we started to make changes. We analyzed what the challenges of the future would be and how we would need to set ourselves up to meet them. We are now working in our new functional setup, which was preceded by a huge process of change, including the creation and filling of some 140 management posts and 600 other positions.

Q. What were the biggest challenges that you faced?

A. When somebody like me, with a background in state politics, joins an international organization like GIZ, some people naturally ask: "Does she know anything about this field of work?" The fact is that I find my horizons being broadened tremendously by my role and the international travel it entails. I am very inquisitive and open by nature, but of course I first had to learn to process all of my new impressions and experiences. That was, and remains, hugely enriching on the one hand, but also challenging on the other. I now notice, after a certain period of time, that I need to go abroad again. I have to find out about our activities on the ground, not least so I get a feel for the real situations in which our field staff live and work.

Q. During the first year, were you sometimes frustrated because things couldn't be changed as quickly as you would have liked?

A. I have a very high frustration threshold. There are, of course, moments when I think: "Did this or that really have to happen on top of everything else?" or "Couldn't we just speed things up a bit?" But I wouldn't really call that frustration. Even when I move forward gradually, it still counts as progress. If I want the end results to be good, I have to give myself and others the necessary time.

Q. Do you think you used your first year in the job as well as you could have?

A. I think that the first year was a good one, despite all the challenges. I tend to strive for perfection, but if I set that aside for one moment, I can definitely say: "Yes, it went well."

Thank you for your time, Ms. Gönner.

About the Deutsche Gesellschaft für Internationale Zusammenarbeit GmbH (GIZ) (www.giz.de)

GIZ is the German government organization that provides a variety of services in the field of international cooperation and economic development. It was established January 1, 2011, through the merger of three prior organizations. GIZ works closely with the German government, European Union institutions, the United Nations, and governments around the world.

GIZ is currently delivering advisory services and projects in more than 130 countries in the following areas: management services; rural development; sustainable infrastructure; security, reconstruction, and peace; social development; governance and democracy; environment and climate change; and economic development and employment.

Interview with Eric Lucas
General Secretary of the Ministry of Justice

Interviewer: Arnauld Bertrand

About Eric Lucas

Eric Lucas currently serves as the secretary general of the Ministry of Justice, a position he has occupied since October 2013. He is a graduate of Sciences Po Paris and the *Ecole du commissariat de la marine*. Before assuming his current position, he served as director of memory, patrimony and archives in the Ministry of Defense from July 2007 to September 2013.

Lucas began his career in 1983 as a commissary on the French destroyer *d'Estrées*. In 1985, he was appointed to the Office of State Action at Sea of the Maritime Prefect for the Mediterranean before returning to operational duty as the commissary of the command and resupply ship *La Marne* in the Indian Ocean. In 1988, he was appointed director of pay services and deputy to the director of the *Commissariat de la Marine* (logistical services to the French Navy). From 1990 to 1995, he served as the Deputy to the Division Chief for Maritime Law at the *Commissariat de la Marine*. In 1995, he was appointed Comptroller General of the Armies, responsible for the judicial unit and ministerial organizational issues. In 1997, Lucas was appointed to the Commission for State Reform as a task leader, a position he held until 1999 when he became deputy to the director of financial affairs in 2000. Between 2004 and 2007, he served as director and secretary general deputy at the Ministry of Defense.

Q. Once you were appointed, how did you prepare to take up your duties?

A. My introduction to my position was very fast, as my predecessor was leaving and his deputy was preparing to leave. I had a great deal of discussion with the deputy general secretary, who remained for three weeks after my arrival, but I had almost no contact with my predecessor.

I figured things out over time. I wanted the agents in the general secretariat to understand that they were being headed by someone who understood their profession. I am the second non-magistrate in this position.

We have monthly meetings with the directors. The first was held the day after my arrival, which allowed me to jump right in.

The cabinet did its best to help me integrate. Relations were cordial and friendly. I was the one who had to define the targets.

They just told me that it was essential for it to work and that the minister's priority was dialogue with the social partners.

- Handovers should be better organized with the predecessor.

- A road map that sets priorities is essential.
- We should organize seminars with feedback and exchange with our peers in order to assure that all Central Administration directors are thoroughly trained to the correct level.
- Possibility for Central Administration directors to choose their direct deputies would be desirable.

Q. Tell us about your first three months in this position.

A. The first week everything is unfamiliar. You explore and try to identify who makes decisions and what decisions are being made.

It takes a few months to come to understand the organization and to see weaknesses.

After three months I understood how the ministry worked, but then the difficulty concerned the core details of the legal and penitentiary professions.

Besides that, everyone here is a magistrate and they all know each other. It's not easy to penetrate this network and decipher its codes. The profession may be too compartmentalized.

Arrival when a term is already underway is not easy, especially when the cabinet is already in place. It was not troublesome in my case because it was the minister's choice. There was an assumed level of risk in bringing in two executives (the secretary general and its deputy) from another ministry.

I did not get to choose my deputy, which would have been more logical; she is anyway an excellent choice.

The minister works most of the time with her cabinet and not with the departments of the Ministry. There is no executive committee (ExCom).

It would be difficult to reduce the size of the cabinets, as politicians are used to it.

- An ExCom that brings together the GS and the CADs would be a step forward.
- The general secretariat should ensure non-policy decision-making.
- Upon arrival, it would be useful to have a road map for the cabinet, and to see the directors to bring you up to speed. There should be a file for taking up duties or a short training period with one's predecessor. It is important to know who you can trust.
- We should organize a training internship for general secretaries after three months with the general secretariat of the government (SGG).
- We should be trained in dialogue with social partners.

Q. Did you have objectives you wished to achieve by the end of your first year in post?

A. I was very busy with three major projects: professional elections, the national platform on legal interceptions, and the office move.

The other main project, if we have time, is to reorganize the general secretariat: what processes, projects, and structures do we need?

We worked quickly on the decree of July 24, on the functioning and role of general secretariats.

The review of missions includes Ministry of Justice projects, dematerialization, and grouping of disputes.

Q. How did you organize your time during the first year?

A. My time was essentially devoted to dialogue with social partners, the implementation of the three major projects I have already mentioned, and also the identification of my administration's weaknesses.

I spent time thinking about how to reorganize the general secretariat.

Given the lack of time to prepare political decisions, things are often done in the urge—we don't have the time or staff to plan ahead.

- The central administration is too weak. There is not enough staff to steer the ministry. The general secretariat must be re-staffed, new posts created, and certain departments centralized.

About the Ministry of Justice

The French judicial system is administered by the Ministry of Justice. It is managed by the minister for justice. The minister lays down the major public policy guidelines in the field of justice, draws up draft laws and regulations, and oversees their implementation. The general secretariat has a number of cross-cutting assignments, including the ministry's modernization strategy, managing human resources, and economic and financial aspects of reforms.

Interview with Michael Roth
Minister of State for Europe at the German Federal Foreign Office

Interviewers: Dr. Fritjof Börner and Birgit Neubert, both EY Germany

About Michael Roth

Michael Roth has been minister of state for Europe at the Federal Foreign Office since December 2013. Since 2014, he has also been the federal government commissioner for Franco German Cooperation. Prior to his present positions, he was a member of the German Bundestag where he served as secretary-general of the SPD in Land-Hesse.

Roth graduated with a degree in political science from the Johann Wolfgang Goethe University of Frankfurt am Main.

Q. How did you prepare for your new role? Did you contact your predecessor?

A. When I was appointed minister of state for Europe in December 2013, I had been a member of the German Bundestag for 15 years and was already well versed in European affairs, which have now become my main responsibility. But of course, working in a large ministry like the Foreign Office with thousands of employees and civil servants was a whole new world.

After I had been appointed, I contacted my predecessor. He belonged to another party, but I knew him well and we had always been on good terms. I asked him what to expect and what the pitfalls were.

I also visited the Foreign Office to get to know my future staff members and find out more about the structures. I have a relatively large team here—an office supervisor, deputy office supervisor, advisors, assistants, etc.!

Q. What did you expect of your new role?

A. I quickly realized that I would have to change my life completely because I would mainly be in Berlin or on business trips and wouldn't be at home in my constituency as much as I used to be. That naturally takes its toll on family life.

Aside from that, I have always understood my position to be very political and wanted that to be reflected in external communications. I believe that is especially important for European issues. Europe is neither a bestseller nor can it be taken for granted—you have to work extremely hard to sell it well. That meant communication had to get better, our public image had to improve, PR had to be stepped up—those were things I resolved to do at the beginning of my term in office. My predecessor attended to a wide range of topics and dossiers. I have always known that Europe is my main responsibility—and that is reflected in my title "Minister of State for Europe."

Q. Speaking of communication, what exactly did you want to change?

A. First of all, I wanted to set clear priorities. I'm responsible for European matters at the Foreign Office. And our external communication should reflect this fact. Instead of nurturing different projects here and there, I dedicate my efforts to selected issues with a clear European dimension. At the moment, this includes first and foremost Greece, but also other topics such as the rule of law, fundamental freedoms, and human rights in the European Union.

Second, I wanted to really step up our use of social media in the form of Twitter and Facebook. None of my predecessors had taken that initiative. I am very active on both accounts, with a little help from my team, of course.

Third, I wanted to significantly intensify our relations with the press. I have a dedicated media relations officer on my team who supports me—in close collaboration with our press office, needless to say. My target group is the younger generation because I believe there is stronger potential among young people to engender pro-European sentiment.

Lastly, I give speeches and lectures as often as possible. One of the topics I am passionate about is the respect for and defense of fundamental freedoms and human rights. I am very active in this area and am involved in various organizations.

Q. How were your first 100 days in office?

A. It was like taking a crash course! It was learning by doing: getting to know colleagues, structures, developing a work routine because it was a bit different to the kind of work I'd done before. As a member of parliament I was my own boss, whereas now as a minister of state I'm part of a more complex organization.

Q. What were the biggest challenges you faced?

A. Setting my own agenda and standards without creating any conflict with other colleagues at the Foreign Office. To be part of a team and a maker at the same time. To be taken seriously and to earn respect—because just as everything was new to me when I took on my new role my colleagues at the Foreign Office had to get used to me and my way of working as well.

Q. Did you have any goals for your first year in office?

A. Yes, I did, but I didn't achieve them all. For example, I aimed to visit every EU member state during my first year in office. That was impossible. I completely underestimated Germany's bilateral obligations. Europe is currently in a perpetual crisis mode, which means, for example, that I have traveled to Greece eight times over the last 18 months, but I haven't been to Slovenia at all yet.

Q. During the first year, were you sometimes frustrated because things couldn't be changed as quickly as you would have liked them to?

A. Yes, of course! This type of work can be extremely frustrating, but it's important not to let frustration get the upper hand. When you do something you enjoy and have high expectations of yourself then you're bound to be disappointed now and again. But you shouldn't let that deter you. If you get bad press for example, or something is communicated incorrectly or you make an appearance that doesn't go as well as it could have. Or if, like me, you have to conduct most of your conversations in English and explain the crisis in Greece with all its economic, social, and political nuances in a foreign language—that's really hard work.

Q. Can you tell us about your working day?

A. I don't have any kind of set working day. Every week is different. I am responsible for relationships with parliament, so when parliament meets, my day is naturally quite different than when I am away traveling, like this week.

I have to be able to familiarize myself with new topics very quickly. For example, Africa is not part of my core portfolio. But it's possible that I will have to answer questions in the Committee on Foreign Affairs about military deployments involving the German armed forces in Africa. I don't have three weeks to prepare when I am told on Monday that I'll be meeting with the committee on Wednesday. Or when we have question time on Wednesday after lunch—then I normally discuss the possible answers with my team on Tuesday. I get a draft from the ministry of course, but I go through all the replies again and make changes if necessary—and these are topics right across the board covering the entire spectrum of international politics. Sometimes you have to have the courage to leave a gap and sometimes you have to bluff your way through, like in every job (laughs). It's important that I can distinguish between what I have to know in detail myself and where I just need to know the right person who has the details.

Q. Do you think you used your first year in the job as well as you could have?

A. I can't say. That's for others to judge. I'm satisfied overall, but there's room for improvement, of course. I'm self-critical enough to see that.

Q. Were there challenges that you should have paid more attention to in hindsight?

A. When I first started, I should have considered more strongly that the Foreign Office is a highly consensus-based ministry that only enters into conflicts when there is a very pressing reason. In my experience there are other ministries that are more willing to engage in conflict, which is also because they deal with issues that are more divisive. Take the Federal Ministry of Labor and the minimum wage debate for example. This kind of political polarization would be very unusual for the Foreign Office with its tradition of diplomacy and continuity.

Thank you for your time Mr. Roth.

About the German Federal Foreign Office

The Federal Foreign Office represents Germany's interests in the world. It promotes international exchange and offers protection and assistance to Germans abroad. With headquarters in Berlin and a network of 229 missions, the Federal Foreign Office maintains Germany's relations with other countries as well as with international and supra-national organizations.

Interview with Christoph Verenkotte
President of the German Federal Office of Administration

Interviewers: Hans-Peter Busson and Birgit Neubert, both EY Germany

About Christoph Verenkotte

Christoph Verenkotte has been the president of the Federal Office of administration since March 1, 2010. Prior to his present position, he was director-general: federal police matters, Federal Ministry of the Interior.

During his career, he has held a variety of senior positions in the Federal Ministry of the Interior and the Federal Office of Administration.

Mr. Verenkotte studied law, history, and philosophy at the University of Bonn. In 1984, he completed his First State Examination in Law, followed by practical training in legal work in Cologne. In 1987, he completed the Second State Examination in Law.

Q. Did you get in touch with your predecessor? If yes, was he able to give you some useful tips?

A. I did get in touch with my predecessor, but that was just part of my preparation. But it was important to get in touch with my predecessor. Why was it important? It was important in order to find out something about the people and working together; for example, about the heads of the directorates general. After a while you have your own—perhaps different—way of seeing things, but it is very helpful when you are starting out because these are not things that you can read up on and you need some kind of starting point.

That is why I tried to talk to as many people as possible who are in contact with the authority. The German Federal Office of Administration (BVA) is a large authority that is involved in a variety of different areas and employs a large number of people. As a result, the BVA also has a lot of external points of contact; for example, with other authorities such as the German Federal Ministry of the Interior, as well as other federal ministries. I am familiar with a number of contacts in this respect, and I was interested to find out how they saw the BVA. This external perspective was very important to me.

I also tried to contact certain internal employees and hold informal discussions with managers and employees. It was important to me to get to know the people who work here.

Q. How did you prepare for your new role?

A. In addition to the discussions and personal contact as I already mentioned, preparing does, of course, also involve taking a look at the details of the position.

In other words, I examined the tasks and topics I would be dealing with, and I tried to do some research and preparation on relevant subjects. I resolved to make some changes with respect to management, leadership, and communication.

Q. What were your expectations in connection with your new role?

A. The BVA is a large authority. The challenges—and also my expectations—were varied. Firstly, there was the wide range of topics, and there was also the structure of the organization. At the time we had 2,500 employees, which has now risen to 4,000. Then there was communication, which I considered to be particularly important because I had found in my previous work that this is an area which is not prioritized enough—at least in the German civil service. Communication plays a very important role, and if you don't focus on it from the very beginning, you are underestimating its importance and will suffer the consequences.

Q. How were your first 100 days in office? Did you have a 100-day plan?

A. I didn't have a 100-day plan, but I did have certain expectations, and there were things that I wanted to achieve in the first 100 days. One thing I can say for sure is that the first 100 days in office are exhausting. I had the advantage that I was familiar with the organization from my previous work. However, I had spent 10 years elsewhere (at the Federal Ministry of the Interior), during which time the organization had changed completely.

Q. What areas did you focus on during the first three months?

A. I was more interested in changing the management, leadership, and communication and less in changing the existing structures.

This meant setting up a staff organization, which the authority did not have before. My predecessor only maintained an informal staff with a limited number of employees. I introduced the staff structures—in the face of significant resistance.

I also introduced a new, open communication process including weekly meetings with the heads of our directorates general followed by the publication of outcomes on the intranet. The weekly meetings were new, the communication of outcomes was new, and publishing them on the intranet was new. The heads of our directorates general had five working days to communicate the outcomes to their managers before they were published on the intranet.

Another new development was that one-on-one meetings were only held with respect to personnel matters, and in all other cases there was always a staff employee on hand to prepare the minutes, document the outcomes, and issue the dated assignments. This constituted a significant cultural shift.

Q. Were target agreement discussions held?

A. They were not, but entirely appropriate controlling was carried out at the level of the directorates general. We had to decide between imposing a completely new system or developing the starting points that were already in place. We opted for the latter. Today we have target agreements with each directorate general, a management system based on key performance indicators, and in addition to the operating organization we have now turned our attention to gradually introducing target agreements in the strategic organization.

Q. Did you communicate your agenda to your managers?

A. I started by communicating the headings. It then transpired that headings can of course be easily misunderstood and are also commented on if you have any intermediaries. Looking back I think I should have communicated in a way that went deeper into the organization and in more detail. That was something that I did wrong.

Q. Was that also how your *2018plus* strategy for your managers and employees came about?

A. The origins of the strategy were different. We realized fairly early on that we would have to communicate on overarching issues in other contexts in order to ensure that we are all pulling together. This gave rise to the weekly meetings with the heads of the directorates general, which are now held every two weeks. We also met twice a year for retreats, which we made a conscious decision to hold outside the BVA. We (the heads of the directorates general and the president and vice presidents) traveled to an external convention center in order to examine issues of collaboration and strategic development. This then led to the *2018plus* strategy. The employees were also involved before the strategy was ratified and published on the Internet. The intention was for everyone to be able to participate and contribute their issues.

Q. Were you able to gain an overview of what "condition" your new area of responsibility was in during the first three months?

A. It's a question of depth. Numbers, dates, facts, and the status of operations are certainly things that you can find out during the first three months, but you have to work at it. But anyone who doesn't make the effort, doesn't question the status quo, and simply lacks the drive as a manager will not be able to do it. Although, the concept of "condition" is always very relative. Our organization is highly varied, and I would not like to fool myself into thinking that I gained a complete overview during the first three months. The sheer variety of issues and tasks makes it impossible.

Q. What were the biggest challenges you faced?

A. There was a significant gap between the organization's very good marketing and the actual situation on the ground. This was something that came to my attention when talking to my external contacts. I decided to approach the issue from two angles, reining in the marketing a bit while also improving the situation internally. But the biggest challenges were the changes to the management and communication culture.

Q. As the president of the German Federal Office of Administration you take an active role in press and public relations work...

A. You are absolutely right. That was a conscious decision on my part because I think it helps us—both with respect to the organization's profile and the discussions we have with the various ministries on future issues. If we do not take a position ourselves on these issues then we will not be taken seriously.

Q. Can you tell us something about the time after you had been in office for about four to six months?

A. That was when I slowly started to realize that I can't do everything all at once. I took on a lot of work at the start, launching a series of projects and tackling various topics—and everyone started complaining after about six months... After all, open communication isn't everything. You also have to make sure that your employees are not overwhelmed. Many quickly start to feel misunderstood with respect to the value attributed to their everyday work. When new projects come along, employees normally react by saying: "But we already have enough to do anyway! Do they have no idea what we do every day, and now this..." New projects are always viewed as being added on top of everything else, and this can become problematic if you don't keep a lid on it and explain the reasons behind it in more detail. This is something that I came to realize, but it is not always easy to implement.

Q. During the first year, were you sometimes frustrated because things could not be changed as quickly as you had perhaps hoped?

A. Yes I was! Definitely! As a manager it is important not to lose touch with your emotions. Otherwise you turn into a machine, which is simply unacceptable. It is important to have an emotional connection to the things that you do. And you also have to have an opinion regarding the value of what you do, which means you have to know why you are doing it, and what you like and what you don't. This is also true for external developments affecting the authority. You have to hold on to your own values, that's very important, in my opinion.

Q. Do you believe that you made the most out of your new role during your first year?

A. To begin with, I was too interested in doing everything all at once. That meant implementing my meta-objectives (new management, new leadership, open and transparent communication) while also getting stuck into the operating issues. This inevitably led to my growing involvement in operating processes. My first year was not ideal in this respect because I should have recognized this and intervened at an earlier stage. That is what I did after the first year. Today I would say: clear interim stages, every three months, in order to assess where we are.

Q. Were there challenges that you believe in retrospect you should have paid more attention to?

A. What I didn't see at first was that the changes I was initiating would lead to a dramatic cultural shift.

Q. Were there also external challenges?

A. I was baffled by a number of things that I considered to be relatively obvious—demographic change, health management, and leadership. Issues that were a reality and where I repeatedly asked myself why not everyone could see them and why more had not been done, both internally and externally.

I also identified a discrepancy between policy and practice. There is also an HR management aspect to this issue, in that increasing numbers of employees at Germany's federal ministries have no practical working experience in other authorities at the federal level. I am a fervent supporter of an exchange between the ministries and other administrative bodies. In Baden-Württemberg and Bavaria it is customary, if not compulsory, to dispose of practical experience in administration for anyone seeking a management position at a ministry as a political functionary. Unfortunately, this has not been the case at the federal level since the mid-1990s. The ministries are increasingly home to a generation of managers who see legislation more as the implementation of political decisions and less as the objective to establish a citizen-centred administration.

Mr. Verenkotte, thank you for talking to us.

About the German Federal Office of Administration (www.bva.bund.de)

The Federal Office of Administration (BVA) is an independent superior federal authority with headquarters in Cologne. BVA is the central service provider of the German federal government. BVA has about 4,000 employees.

The founding principle of BVA is to take over administrative tasks of German federal ministries, to centralize them, and perform them more effectively. Current key areas of cross-cutting tasks include IT services and products, personnel recruitment, travel management, and the processing of renumeration and allowances.

About the Interviewers

Arnauld Bertrand is an Advisory Partner of Ernst & Young et Associés based in Paris (France). He also serves as EY Global Government & Public Sector (GPS) Advisory Leader and World Bank Account International Leader. Previously, Arnauld Bertrand has led GPS activities for the French, Luxemburg, and Maghreb EY regions and was the EY Global Public Finance Management (PFM) Leader. (arnauld.bertrand@fr.ey.com)

Dr. Fritjof Börner is a Partner of Ernst & Young GmbH Wirtschaftsprüfungsgesellschaft and Global Client Service Partner for the German Federal Government. He serves clients in IP/IT Law and has 20 years of experience working in the public sector. Prior to joining EY, Fritjof was In-House Counsel at Bertelsmann AG. (fritjof.boerner@de.ey.com)

Hans-Peter Busson is a Partner of Ernst & Young GmbH Wirtschaftsprüfungsgesellschaft and Government & Public Sector Assurance Leader for Germany, Switzerland and Austria. He is a public auditor and tax advisor and has more than 20 years of experience in the public sector. Hans-Peter also serves as EY's Global ECA Coordination Leader. (hans-peter.busson@de.ey.com)

Birgit Neubert is a Senior Manager of Ernst & Young GmbH Wirtschaftsprüfungsgesellschaft and Government & Public Sector Brand, Marketing and Communications Leader for Germany, Switzerland and Austria. She has extensive experience in the public sector as well as in media and communications. (birgit.neubert@de.ey.com)

Index of Interviewers and Interviewees

A
Abramson, Mark A., 176
Adelstein, Jonathan S., 47, 49, 66, 128–130
Appel, Peter H., 20, 35, 123
Ashe, Daniel M., 68, 112, 136–137

B
Babbitt, Randy, 103
Berry, John, 35, 54–55, 67, 76, 134, 137
Bertrand, Arnauld, 146, 148–149, 151, 159, 170
Birnbaum, Elizabeth, 114
Blank, Rebecca M., 28, 69, 74–75, 121–123
Börner, Fritjof, 153, 156, 161, 170
Borras, Rafael, 64, 70–71, 90
Bromwich, Michael R., 16, 70, 110–112, 114
Busson, Hans–Peter, 165, 170
Butler, J. Dudley, 115

C
Corr, William V., 88, 90
Criscitello, Doug, 138

D
DeSeve, G. Edward, 16, 135, 138

F
Faure, Pascal, 149–150
Filippini, Jérôme, 71, 151–153

G
Gallagher, Patrick D., 55–56, 63, 75, 120–121, 124
Gehb, Jürgen, 41–42, 69, 153–156
Gibson, Sloan D., 33, 43, 68, 84, 93
Gönner, Tanja, 156–158
Gould, W. Scott, 63–64, 86, 91
Groshen, Erica L., 25, 32–33, 41, 47, 71, 124

H
Hamburg, Margaret A., 22, 36, 50, 63, 65, 79, 113, 115
Harris, Seth D., 44, 56–57, 59, 64, 91
Hayes, David J., 85, 91
Hickey, Allison A., 18, 39, 42, 57–59, 100, 103
Higginbottom, Heather, 25, 92
Hightower, Dennis F., 33, 42, 92
Hinson, David A., 65, 70, 135, 139
Hopper, Abigail Ross, 20, 42, 115
Huerta, Michael P., 20, 22–23, 42, 71, 75, 104
Huther, Brad, 48, 139
Hyde, Pamela S., 46, 49, 56, 66, 135, 139

J

Jefferson, Raymond M., 65, 135, 140
Jones, Maurice, 15, 57, 92

K

Kappos, David J., 17, 38, 40, 48, 50, 58, 67, 98–99, 101, 104
Kennedy, TJ, 36, 104
Kerlikowske, R. Gil, 24–25, 69, 77, 105

L

Lawrence, Paul R., 175
Lu, Christopher P., 59, 76, 86, 93
Lucas, Eric, 40, 159–161

M

Macfarlane, Allison M., 42–43, 110, 116
Mader, David, 134, 140
Main, Joseph A., 16, 111–112, 116
Majumdar, Arun, 63–64, 67, 129–130
Mayorkas, Alejandro N., 34, 57–59, 75, 99, 105
McNutt, Marcia K., 39, 46, 69–70, 120–122, 124
Mendez, Victor M., 66–67, 75, 93, 128, 131
Merrigan, Kathleen A., 41, 43, 46, 94
Miller, Anthony W., 28, 58, 94
Morton, John T., 22, 50, 68, 105

N

Neubert, Birgit, 153, 156, 161, 165, 170
Newell, Richard G., 38, 55, 63, 120, 122, 125
Nides, Thomas R., 94

P

Petzel, Robert A., 106
Pistole, John S., 18, 57, 100, 106
Poneman, Daniel B., 54, 62–63, 87, 95
Porcari, John D., 39, 47, 95

R

Rodriguez, Leon, 34, 46–47, 106
Rogoff, Peter M., 131
Rosekind, Mark R., 22–23, 35, 51, 76, 116
Roth, Michael, 34, 46, 161–164
Roy, Delphine, 151
Runcie, James W., 17, 48, 51, 100, 107

S

Stevens, David H., 16, 29, 33, 48–49, 51, 55, 101, 107
Strickland, David L., 49, 111–112, 117
Suh, Rhea, 39–40, 140
Sullivan, Kathryn D., 34, 41, 76, 122, 125
Szabo, Joseph C., 129, 131

T

Taggart, William J., 15, 17, 28, 51, 64, 66, 98, 101, 107
Tenenbaum, Inez Moore, 39, 64, 110–112, 117
Thompson, John H., 22–23, 49, 71, 125

V

Verenkotte, Christoph, 51, 165–169

W

Wakefield, Mary K., 40, 62, 67, 75, 136, 141
Wellinghoff, Jon B., 56, 110, 117
Whitaker, Michael G., 16, 25, 65, 108

References

Achenbach, Joel, *A Hole at the Bottom of the Sea: The Race to Kill the BP Oil Gusher.* New York: Simon & Schuster, 2011.

Bair, Sheila, *Bull by the Horns: Fighting to Save Main Street from Wall Street and Wall Street from Itself.* New York: Free Press, 2012.

Bernanke, Ben S., *The Courage to Act: A Memoir of a Crisis and Its Aftermath.* New York: W.W. Norton & Company, 2015.

Broder, John M. and Matthew Wald, "Chairman of the NRC to Resign Under Fire." *The New York Times,* April 20, 2011.

Fox, Tom, "The Federal Coach." *The Washington Post,* September 6, 2013.

Geithner, Timothy, *Stress Test: Reflections on Financial Crises.* New York: Crown Publishers, 2014.

Kappos, David, "Government Disservice: Overcoming Washington Dysfunction to Improve Congressional Stewardship of the Executive Branch." Panel discussion at the Partnership for Public Service, Washington, D.C., September 17, 2015.

Keegan, Michael, "Pursuing an Opportunity Agenda: A Conversation with Nani Coloretti, Deputy Secretary, U.S. Department of Housing and Urban Development." *The Business of Government,* Fall 2015.

Layton, Lyndsey, "Duncan exerts influence while he has some." *The Washington Post,* July 9, 2015.

Markon, Jerry, "This man has to help fix one of Washington's most difficult agencies," *The Washington Post,* June 4, 2015.

McGlone, Peggy, "King of the Castle." *The Washington Post,* September 30, 2015a.

McGlone, Peggy, "New Smithsonian chief takes the grand tour." *The Washington Post,* July 8, 2015b.

Nixon, Ron, "Consumer Safety Chief Leaves a Small Agency with Bigger Powers." *The New York Times,* November 30, 2013.

Nixon, Ron, "Senate Confirms Ex-Security Aide, an Africa Expert, as Head of U.S.A.I.D." *The New York Times,* December 1, 2105.

Palmer, Doug, "Obama pick for deputy Commerce job to withdraw." Reuters, September 28, 2011.

Peters, Katherine McIntire, "Wasteland: Decades of Poor Management at the Energy Department Threatens Public Health and National Security." *Government Executive*, December 2010.

Rein, Lisa and Joe Davidson, "Director of OPM Resigns Under Fire." *The Washington Post,* June 11, 2015.

Rubin, Rita, "Margaret A. Hamburg, MD, Reflects on 6 Years at FDA." *JAMA: The Journal of the American Medical Association* Vol 313, No. 23 (June 16, 2015).

Samuelson, Darren, "Obama's vanishing administration." *Politico*, January 5, 2016.

Springer, Linda, "Building Relationships: Three Conversations to Have Right Away," in Paul Lawrence and Mark Abramson, *Paths to Making a Difference: Leading in Government (Revised Edition)*. Lanham: Rowman and Littlefield Publishers, 2013.

About the Authors

Paul R. Lawrence is a Principal in the Advisory Services practice of Ernst & Young LLP, and a leader in its Federal Government Consulting Practice. He served as the Partner-in-Charge of the Ernst & Young Initiative on Leadership, which resulted in the publication of this book.

Lawrence has more than 25 years of experience working closely with government leaders. Prior to joining Ernst & Young LLP, Lawrence was a Vice President with Accenture, an Executive Director with the MITRE Corporation, a Vice President with IBM Business Consulting Services, and a Partner at PricewaterhouseCoopers.

He has written extensively on technology, management, and government. He is the co-author of *What Government Does: How Political Executives Manage, Paths to Making a Difference: Leading in Government,* and the co-editor of *Transforming Organizations* and *Learning the Ropes: Insights for Political Appointees*. He has testified before Congress and several state legislatures. He serves on the Board of Advisors to the Economic Program at the University of Massachusetts and has served on the Board of Advisors of the Thomas Jefferson Public Policy Program at The College of William and Mary. He was twice selected by *Federal Computer Week* as one of the top 100 public service business leaders. He is a Fellow of the National Academy of Public Administration.

Lawrence earned his Master of Arts and Ph.D. in economics from Virginia Tech. He earned his Bachelor of Arts degree in economics from the University of Massachusetts, Amherst, graduating Phi Beta Kappa.

Mark A. Abramson is President of Leadership Inc. He served as Project Director of the Ernst & Young Initiative on Leadership.

During his career, Abramson has served as Executive Director of the IBM Center for The Business of Government, President of the Council for Excellence in Government, and a Senior Program Evaluator in the Office of the Assistant Secretary for Planning and Evaluation in the Department of Health and Human Services. While at the Council for Excellence in Government, Abramson was instrumental in launching *The Prune Book* series in 1988, which profiled the toughest jobs in government.

Throughout his career, Abramson has published numerous books and articles. He is the co-author of *Paths to Making a Difference: Leading in Government* and *What Government Does: How Political Executives Manage,* and co-editor of *The Operator's Manual for the New Administration, Getting It Done: A Guide for Government Executives,* and *Learning the Ropes: Insights for Political Appointees.* He is also the author or editor of 16 books and has published more than 100 articles on public management. From 2005 to 2008, he served on the editorial board of the *Public Administration Review* as Case Study Editor. He has also served as a Contributing Editor to *Government Executive* and as a member of the Board of Editors and Forum Editor for *The Public Manager.*

Abramson was elected a Fellow of the National Academy of Public Administration and is past President of the National Capital Area Chapter (NCAC) of the American Society for Public Administration. He received a Master of Arts degree in political science from the Maxwell School of Citizenship and Public Affairs at Syracuse University and a Bachelor of Arts degree from Florida State University.

About EY

EY | Assurance | Tax | Transactions | Advisory

About EY

EY is a global leader in assurance, tax, transaction and advisory services. The insights and quality services we deliver help build trust and confidence in the capital markets and in economies the world over. We develop outstanding leaders who team to deliver on our promises to all of our stakeholders. In so doing, we play a critical role in building a better working world for our people, for our clients and for our communities.

EY refers to the global organization, and may refer to one or more of the member firms of Ernst & Young Global Limited, each of which is a separate legal entity. Ernst & Young Global Limited, a UK company limited by guarantee, does not provide services to clients. For more information about our organization, please visit ey.com.

Ernst & Young LLP is a client-serving member firm of Ernst & Young Global Limited operating in the US.

© 2016 Ernst & Young LLP.
All Rights Reserved.

SCORE no. BT0575